BLASPHEMY
AND THE
BATTLE FOR FAITH

BLASPHEMY AND THE BATTLE FOR FAITH

F. LaGard Smith

HODDER AND STOUGHTON

LONDON SYDNEY AUCKLAND TORONTO

All scripture quotations in this book are taken from the Holy Bible, New International Version, Copyright © 1973, 1978, 1984 by the International Bible Society.

British Library Cataloguing in Publication Data
Smith, F. LaGard
  Blasphemy and the battle for faith.
  1. Great Britain. Blasphemy
  I. Title
  291.5'60'5

ISBN 0-340-52279-8

Copyright c 1990 by F. LaGard Smith. First printed 1990. All rights reserved. No part of this publication may be reproduced or transmitted in any form or by any means, electronically or mechanically, including photocopying, recording or any information storage or retrieval system, without either prior permission in writing from the publisher or a licence permitting restricted copying. In the United Kingdom such licences are issued by the Copyright Licensing Agency, 33–34 Alfred Place, London WC1E 7DP. Typeset by Selectmove Ltd. Printed in Great Britain for Hodder & Stoughton Limited, Mill Road, Dunton Green, Sevenoaks, Kent by Richard Clay Ltd, Bungay, Suffolk.

Hodder & Stoughton Editorial Office: 47 Bedford Square, London WC1B 3DP.

Dedicated to the battle for faith in a nation struggling for spiritual survival, and to a greater sense of the sacred in us all.

With appreciation to Professor Harold Bigham, Mandy Brown, Ian Ferrier Esq, Dr Michael Gose, Bruce Hughes, Clifford Joseph Esq, and Steven Masood.

My special thanks to Jerry E. Jones and J. David Pawson for their insightful contributions to this book.

Contents

Prologue — 9
1. In the Wake of Rushdie — 11
2. Blasphemy Through Islamic Eyes — 21
3. Just What Is Blasphemy? — 39
4. Can Non-Christians Be Ignored? — 51
5. Second Thoughts About Blasphemy — 61
6. At What Cost Free Speech? — 75
7. Whether to Abolish — 89
8. Blasphemy on the Screen — 100
9. Blasphemy Among Bishops — 114
10. 'Theological Blasphemy' — 130
11. Sacrilege By Saints — 147
12. 'New Age' Blasphemy — 168
13. The Language of Blasphemy — 186
14. Jesus the Blasphemer — 196
15. Towards a Godly Intolerance — 209

PROLOGUE

On February 14th, 1989, Iran's fundamentalist leader, the late Ayatollah Khomeini, broadcast the following statement on Tehran Radio: 'I inform the proud Muslim people of the world that the author of *The Satanic Verses* book, which is against Islam, the Prophet and the Koran, and all involved in its publication, are sentenced to death.' The author, award-winning novelist Salman Rushdie, denied that his book, published in 1988 by Viking Penguin Books, was a blasphemy against Islam.

Massive demonstrations by Muslims around the world lent widespread support to the Ayatollah's death threat. British Muslims, who had protested previously by burning a copy of *The Satanic Verses*, clearly backed the worldwide protests, but were divided on the response they should make to the sentence against Rushdie. According to the Ayatollah, 'All Muslims' were urged to execute Mr Rushdie and his publishers 'wherever they find them'.

Leading British Muslims expressed the belief that the executions could not be carried out in violation of British laws, but have sought (so far unsuccessfully) to bring criminal charges against Mr Rushdie under Britain's centuries-old, but rarely-enforced blasphemy laws. Common law blasphemy in England punishes contempt only against the Christian religion, in keeping with the constitutional ties to the established Church of England.

Despite continued calls for the book to be banned, *The Satanic Verses* has been a steady best-seller from the very inception of what now has come to be known as 'the Rushdie affair'. Following the death of Khomeini in June 1989, the Ayatollah's Iranian successors have reassured the world that the Ayatollah's death sentence against Mr Rushdie remains intact. Mr Rushdie, author of the novels *Grimus*, *Midnight's Children*, and *Shame*, among other books and television films, continues in hiding at the time of this writing.

The many issues raised about Britain's blasphemy laws in the wake of the Rushdie affair are discussed in the first half of this book. Particular emphasis has been given to how Muslims and Christians, respectively, have viewed blasphemy both throughout history and in the context of current events.

The second, and more important, half of the book addresses blasphemy and sacrilege as they relate to all of us in the broader context of both secular society and the Church. On a very personal level, quite apart from dramatic death threats and stormy public demonstrations, each of us ultimately is caught up in the issue of blasphemy. Whether because of casual attitudes towards that which is sacred, or profane words which fall thoughtlessly from our lips, or human doctrines which have been elevated to the level of Biblical truth, the challenge of this book is to rediscover a God who deserves to be taken more seriously.

1

In the Wake of Rushdie

Rethinking the Issue of Blasphemy

> Whispered insinuations are the rhetoric of the devil.
>
> J.W. von Goethe

Could it be that Salman Rushdie and the late Ayatollah Khomeini have unwittingly opened a window of crucial dialogue for the Christian community? Have they together given us a unique opportunity to explore the rarely discussed issue of blasphemy and its more far-reaching question as to how seriously we take our religion? Beyond the headline, '*Satanic Verses* Brings Death Sentence to Rushdie', and the sense of outrage which civilised governments and people around the world expressed in response, are more serious implications for both the legal system and the Church.

As an author, my concern for freedom of expression puts me solidly with Salman Rushdie. It sends chills down my spine to think that something I happen to write in the quiet reverie of my Cotswold cottage retreat could turn out to be the cause for political banishment, criminal imprisonment, or – God forbid – a bullet of hatred fired into my brain. It is simply inconceivable that the sharing of one's ideas, whether fact or fiction, should produce such radical responses.

As one who also wears the hat of an American law professor, I am well aware of the ongoing need for vigilance in maintaining free speech and a free press. No society stifling the free flow of ideas can call itself truly democratic. If limits must be set on public expression and publication (such as malicious libel or immediate threat to national security), those limits must be justified by compelling reasons at every turn.

Yet as a conscientious Christian, I am in sympathy with Muslims the world over whose sense of outrage at blasphemy within the context of Islam led them to outspoken defiance. It hardly mattered that few of them had read even the offensive portions of *The Satanic Verses*. What mattered was that they perceived a callous contempt directed against their faith, and they reacted to it as if it really mattered.

Certainly, many Muslims would have killed Salman Rushdie for his book (in Islam a traitor to Allah is to be killed). Yet, at least they care about what they believe – *really* care. If, as twentieth-century Christians, we pride ourselves on the fact that we should not kill another person for his ideas, no matter how repugnant, can we with equal force say that we care about our professed Christian faith – *really* care?

Some might suggest, of course, that our outwardly tepid reaction to blasphemy against Christian belief is no more than a difference of temperament and culture when contrasted with Muslims. They would say that we care just as much as Muslims do, but express our concern through avenues which are less visibly demonstrative. Whether that is a valid distinction remains to be seen. Is our society in some way more 'civilised' when it comes to venting public outrage, or is the truth of the matter that we simply do *not* care about religion to the same degree?

Does it offend us, for example, when television and movie dialogue contains a constant flow of profane references to God and Jesus Christ? Indeed, do we find casual references to deity spilling profanely from our own lips throughout the course of a day? What is our reaction to such presentations as *The Life of Brian*, or *The Last Temptation of Christ*? It is altogether possible that we have lauded their theatrical virtues and thereby unwittingly lent our personal approval to a *cheapening* of the ultimate divine drama. It is also possible that we have found ourselves laughing at humour contemptuously directed at the incarnate God and those sincere believers who have placed their faith in him.

If we have found such presentations distasteful, we nevertheless may have shrugged them aside as just so much drivel. Or, to the contrary, we may have felt an urgent sense of outrage. If so, have we really struggled with ways in which we ought to protest at the affront they make to Christian faith?

Far more important are questions which relate to the dwindling ranks of active believers within the Christian fellowship, and to a Church which is both torn by division and threatened with premature demise by a malaise of indifference. Does it bother us when Church leaders and Christian scholars scoff at the miracle stories of the Gospel narratives? Are we alarmed when the Church *appears* to be concerned only about political and social issues and lacking any concern about the eternal questions of sin and salvation?

Even if we truly are sensitive to these issues, perhaps we need to rethink our priorities. Interesting, isn't it, that apparently we are more outraged when a homosexual-run newspaper contemptuously vilifies the person of Jesus than when a leading Anglican bishop denies the virgin birth and bodily resurrection of Jesus? The former is taken as blasphemous while the latter is perceived as simply a scholarly difference of opinion.

One might argue that we have focused on the lesser evil. Surely, there can be no doubt as to which has the greater potential for the broadest publicity, or from which source one might least expect a broadside to Christian faith, or which promises more lasting damage to Christianity. Perhaps we have too easily confused blasphemy (speaking irreverently of God and sacred things) and heresy (espousing opinions contrary to orthodox tenets of a given religion). Perhaps we are even confused as to which is the more serious threat to faith.

Questions at Every Turn

Of the myriad questions begging to be answered, perhaps the most troubling is, just what is blasphemy? Even that question must be prefaced by the issues of who should decide, and upon what basis the definition will be determined. Assuming that we could *define* blasphemy in some way agreeable to all, the next question would be whether society ought to maintain laws *punishing* it. Perhaps society would be better off abolishing blasphemy laws altogether.

But, if blasphemy laws are kept on the books, surely they must be extended to religions other than the Christian faith, as many today are urging. Traditionally, of course, blasphemy has been viewed solely through the eyes of the established Church of England, but in a pluralistic society there is more than one view of blasphemy to be considered. In the wake of the outcry over the Rushdie affair, one would be hard pressed to deny that people of other religions can be equally offended.

Unfortunately, the issues are not as clear cut as either abolishing the blasphemy laws or extending them to non-Christians. Some people think it is desirable to keep blasphemy laws on the books, just as they are, but without actively enforcing them. Their idea is that even unenforced blasphemy laws could 'make a public statement' about the seriousness of religious libel. Others would fear the potential for abuse, should a prosecutor decide to engage in discriminatory selective enforcement.

Apart from legal concerns and difficult questions of enforceability, the issue becomes more personal for the Christian community. What should be our response to blasphemy? Many believe that calling attention to blasphemy merely serves to enhance public awareness all the more. They suggest, for example, that the film *The Last Temptation of Christ* would have died for lack of interest in the absence of concerted Christian protest. Faced with such possibilities, how can we as individual Christians make a difference when faced with blasphemy and high-handed heresy?

These and other significant issues will be the object of our concern in the remaining pages of this book. Beyond that, our review of the questions involved will lead us, hopefully, to an even greater appreciation for the sanctity of faith and for the reverence due the God of all Creation. By the very nature of blasphemy, the ground upon which we proceed is indeed holy ground!

Blasphemy, an Old Story

We are not, of course, the first people ever to struggle with the meaning and significance of blasphemy or impertinence before God. Even the polytheistic Greeks condemned their blasphemers. Their concern, of course, was not quite as noble as outrage at irreverence. It was simply a pragmatic fear for the safety of the community if the wrath of the gods was stirred by giving them offence. Thus attempting self-protection, Periclean Greece prosecuted Anaxagoras the philosopher, who had the boldness to suggest that there might be a superior intellect that had imposed a purposeful order in the universe. The idea of such a 'Creator' surely offended the lesser gods! The sculptor Phidias was thought to have profaned Athena when he carved a figure of himself on the shield of her statue. Mixture of the holy and the profane has always begged for trouble.

More in the nature of heresy, perhaps, was the case of Euripides, the tragic poet, who dared to doubt the sanctity of oaths witnessed by the gods. Or take the military general, Alcibiades, who mocked the religious rites honouring Demeter, the grain goddess. Or indeed -Protagoras, the famous mathematician, who confessed outright to being an agnostic. How easily we have moved over the centuries from blasphemy to heresy to apostasy!

Of course, the most famous case of blasphemy, other than the trial of Jesus Christ himself, resulted in the execution of Socrates. His blasphemy lay in corrupting the youth of Athens by disbelieving the state gods and advocating his own deities. His case forcefully demonstrates that 'blasphemy' is not always derisive language hurled against deity. It may be merely the preference for one deity over another.

Closer to Home

As a variation on theme, blasphemy may also be no greater crime than having a different understanding of the same God. Nowhere has this been illustrated more tragically than in the bloodstained history of the Christian faith. For medieval Catholics, Protestantism itself was heresy, punishable by death. Tutored accordingly by the Catholics, Protestants themselves soon began redefining blasphemy as anything with which *they* happened to disagree! Martin Luther, for example, turned the tables by condemning as blasphemy the persecution of Protestants by Catholics. As Luther saw it, the sin of blasphemy was also committed in questioning God's judgments, or merely missing church services!

Calvin, too, was not far behind. In 1553, his enclave at Geneva executed Micheal Servetus for anti-trinitarian beliefs – beliefs which were said to be 'horrible blasphemies' that scandalised the Trinity. In one of the most interesting of all blasphemy cases, Ferenc David, head of Transylvania's Unitarian Church, was convicted of blasphemy by the Hungarian Diet for urging that Christians should not worship Christ!

Incredibly, ranting and raving could also lead one to the gallows under the condemnation of blasphemy, at least if you were one of the Ranters targeted by an Act of Parliament in 1650. Because the Ranters believed that God's grace was boundless, and that therefore nothing is sinful, they incurred the wrath of the state by being as flagrantly obscene and blasphemous as possible. Although England was somewhat more merciful to convicted Ranters, Scotland gave them an early opportunity to test their theory of boundless mercy – at the end of a rope!

Need we also mention George Fox, the founding Quaker, who was prosecuted four times for blasphemy because of his belief in 'Christ within'? Or William Penn, imprisoned for being an anti-trinitarian? Even after the Toleration Act of 1689, blasphemy remained punishable by the state. And that blasphemy included blasphemy-as-heresy, whether against the Christian faith generally, or against the teachings of the established Church in particular.

Not even in the American colonies was the thirst for blasphemy prosecutions assuaged. The Virginia laws of 1611 called for the death penalty where there was blasphemy against either Christianity or the Trinity. Most of the other colonies also fell into line, but gradually lessened the punishment to imprisonment, banishment, fines, whipping and branding. Just as in Europe, sectarianism itself was deemed to be blasphemy, as seen, for example, when the Quakers were regarded as blasphemers by the Puritan reformers in Massachusetts.

During the Age of Enlightenment in the eighteenth century, the passion for prosecuting blasphemy subsided, with only a couple of dozen convictions taking place on either side of the Atlantic. Among them were: the Unitarian minister whose book argued that Christ was subordinate to God; a Bible scholar who questioned the literal interpretation of miracles; and the publishers of other books deemed to be equally heretical.

Shocked by Others' Outrage

This brief review of blasphemy sounds like ancient history until we are shocked into the present by an Islamic death sentence pronounced against a modern British author. Some would dismiss such a death threat as simply a political ploy conceived by a weakened Iranian leader in an attempt to solidify his support base. Others would see it as part of a religion which unashamedly condones violence, in contrast to Christianity which, despite the wholesale shedding of blood at the hands of Christians over the centuries, unequivocally condemns violence.

At least one commentator wonders if what we are witnessing is not simply a phase of immaturity through which a major religion goes in what might be regarded as its hyperactive teenage years. *The Times*'s religious affairs editor, Clifford Longley, suggests this interesting parallel:

> The outlook of Islam in the twentieth century is not

so different from that of Christianity in the thirteenth or fourteenth. Indeed, many scholars regard Islam as going through a period in many respects analogous to Europe's own medieval era. The dates fit this analogy: Islam is approximately 600 years younger than Christianity, and is now beginning its fifteenth century.

The fate of a European author who insulted the honour and chastity of Christ 600 years ago does not bear thinking about (*The Times*, February 15th, 1989).

However we might explain it, our sense of shock remains. And the fact that we should feel such shock is extremely interesting. It is not as if God himself has never imposed the death penalty for blasphemy, for we know that just the opposite is true. At a time predating both Christianity and Islam, the God of Israel commanded death for blasphemy:

> . . . anyone who blasphemes the name of the LORD must be put to death. The entire assembly must stone him. Whether an alien or native-born, when he blasphemes the Name, he must be put to death (Lev. 24:16).

Nor is it simply as if Christ ushered in a new era of love for one's enemies which, all too simplistically, we sometimes have interpreted as divine repeal of any death penalty whatever. (The cross was the *supreme* death penalty!) No, vastly more important, I suggest, is yet another explanation for our sense of shock at what seems to be such radical behaviour on the part of Islam's leaders.

Somewhere along the way, as a Christian people *we have lost our sense of moral outrage*. We've shied away from righteous indignation. In a live-and-let-live spirit of what seems to be Christian tolerance, we've not only turned the other cheek to those who dishonour God, but turned our eyes away as well. The cause of our shock, then, may be much more than the late Ayatollah's grandstanding death threat itself. The fact is that most of us no longer appreciate fully what it means to take religion seriously.

Is our indifference to moral and religious outrage symptomatic of an underlying cancer of indifference to God himself? If so, the issue is not occasional guerrilla-strike blasphemy, or shocking death threats to insensitive authors, or even whether the blasphemy laws ought to be extended to non-Christians. The issue for Christians is personal commitment. The issue is holiness. The issue, even in a sophisticated twentieth century, is humble reverence and awe before the majestic God of the universe.

Can we find a way to recapture it? Can we begin to understand that the greater blasphemy is our own indifference to our Maker?

2

Blasphemy Through Islamic Eyes

Lessons From a Misunderstood Religion?

> Orthodoxy is my doxy; heterodoxy is another man's doxy.
>
> William Warburton
> (Remark to Lord Sandwich)

Whoever would have guessed that as far distant from the Middle Ages as 1989 a novelist writing in England would be the object of a death threat from the leader of another country for including an offensive piece of fiction in his book? It would be one thing if as a literary work *The Satanic Verses* was universally recognised as being worth all the excitement, but, despite its patches of brilliance and often keen insight, it has not generally received full marks.

It hardly matters that the author received a record-breaking cash advance from his publisher, nor that the book was touted by its promoters as 'this great wheel of a book', nor even that the notoriety of the Ayatollah's death threat rocketed the book on to the best-seller list.

If you listen to many critics, the book itself might well have deserved an early demise for being stylistically halting and overly cumbersome. But a *death sentence* for its author?

Such a threat was all the more curious because of the fact that, pursuant to Islamic law, one may not be sentenced to death without a trial and an opportunity to retract the blasphemy.

Salman Rushdie had been given neither. Nor was he a citizen of Iran, from which the Ayatollah issued the decree. Nor (as is consistent with our own law) does just any Muslim have the right to carry out a death penalty, as called for by Khomeini. Nevertheless, the sentence stood, and Rushdie was forced to seek (and was given) the protection of the police, whom, adding irony to irony, he reviles and characterises in his book as racist thugs.

One could see trouble brewing. In fact, Mr Khushwant Singh, the Indian editor of the book's publisher, Viking-Penguin Press, gave an unheeded warning that failure to edit offensive portions of *The Satanic Verses* would bring mayhem. You also knew something must have been wrong when the book was banned in Bangladesh, Egypt and Saudi Arabia. In Indonesia, too, officials feared it might destabilise the country, and in Singapore, where pressure from Malaysian Muslims was exerted, the book was banned for 'denigrating a major religion and its prophet'.

Interestingly, *The Satanic Verses* is about a fictional character very much like Salman Rushdie himself, a person caught between his roots in Bombay and his adopted culture in England. The focus is on an immigrant family in London's East End, a Muslim Imam exiled in a Kensington flat, and the roots of Islam – all of which are things which, from his Indian background, Rushdie understood very well.

No Cause For Surprise

Indeed, it is obvious that Salman Rushdie himself appreciated the potential for serious personal harm to anyone who blasphemes Islam. (By my count, variations of the word *blasphemy* appear no less than fourteen times in the book, often with reference to blasphemy against Muhammad or Islam.) The following passages from *The Satanic Verses* are uncannily prophetic:

> Baal asked: 'Why are you sure he will kill you?'
> Salman the Persian answered: 'It's his Word against mine' (p. 368).

> Mahound [the Prophet] shakes his head. 'Your blasphemy, Salman, can't be forgiven. Did you think I wouldn't work it out? To set your words against the Words of God' (p. 374).

> 'Salman,' the Prophet wishes to know. 'Has he been found?'
> 'Not yet. He's hiding; but it won't be long' (p. 373).

Could Mr Rushdie have been so blind to the realities of his own contrived fiction? As one who studied Islam as part of his courses at Cambridge, was he not keenly aware that choosing to call the Prophet 'Mahound' echoed the slander of medieval European detractors who called Muhammad by this name as synonymous with the devil? (In fact, Rushdie acknowledges this obvious association through the words of one of the characters in *The Satanic Verses*, who says, 'a wronged man, his name, like that of Muhammad-Mahon-Mahound, a synonym for evil . . .' p. 401.)

Did Rushdie not know that he was in dangerous territory to suggest that Muhammad's 'revelation' was conveniently received from Gabriel only after Muhammad had already decided upon a particular course of action? (How 'well timed the angel's revelations tended to be . . . All those revelations of convenience . . . Mahound had no time for scruples . . . no qualms about ends and means . . .' pp. 364, 365, 363.)

Was it not inviting violent reaction to suggest that the Qur'an was the sometimes-purposely-distorted product of one of the Prophet's scribes, whose suspicions led him to test the authenticity of the claimed revelations? ('Mahound did not notice the alterations. So there I was, actually writing the Book, or re-writing, anyway, polluting the word of God with my own profane language' p. 367.)

Did he think he could escape with impunity after the story of the twelve prostitutes, each of whom took on the name of one of Muhammad's twelve wives in order to titillate their customers better? ('Strangest of all was the whore who had taken the name of "Zainab bint Khuzaimah", knowing that this wife of Mahound had recently died. The necrophilia of her lovers, who forbade her to make any movements, was one of the more unsavoury aspects of the new regime at The Curtain' p. 382.)

Was it a harmless bit of fiction that led Rushdie to suggest that Muhammad was a sex-crazed man of God? ('After his [first] wife's death Mahound was no angel, you understand my meaning' p. 366.)

There seems to be little question but that the book is offensive. During the initial uproar over the Rushdie affair, Sir Geoffrey Howe said of *The Satanic Verses*,

> It's a book that is offensive in many other ways as well. The British Government, the British people don't have any affection for the book. The book is extremely critical and rude about us. It compares Britain with Hitler's Germany. We don't like that

any more than the people of the Moslem faith like the attack on their faith contained in the book (News sources, March 3rd, 1989).

Indeed, Margaret Thatcher is referred to with the greatest of disrespect as 'Mrs Torture' and 'Maggie the Bitch' (pp. 266, 269).

Writer Roald Dahl, in a letter to *The Times* (February 28th, 1989), shared Sir Geoffrey's sentiments, denouncing Rushdie as a 'dangerous opportunist'.

> Clearly he has profound knowledge of the Muslim religion and its people, and he must have been totally aware of the deep and violent feelings his book would stir up among devout Muslims. In other words, he knew exactly what he was doing and he cannot plead otherwise.

What Rushdie did *not* expect, of course, was that a prominent mullah and statesman would bring his influence to bear in such a dramatic fashion.

Dangerous opportunist? Offensive? Intentionally insensitive? *Blasphemous*? For which of these charges would an author be subject to the death penalty? In our society, of course, the correct answer is 'None'. In the society from which the threat came, however, blasphemy is indeed a capital offence.

Why Such Furore?

Of course, the death penalty has to be put into its proper context. In the same week as the death threat to Rushdie, Iran executed eighty-one people for drug trafficking, bringing to nearly eight hundred the number hanged on criminal charges in one year alone. One could argue that blasphemy, as a pollution of the soul, deserves at least as serious a punishment as pollution of the body through illegal drugs.

Then again, thousands were put to death during the Ayatollah's regime, most of whom died for no reason other than that they were political enemies of the state. Life becomes cheap in the hands of a tyrant – Muslim or otherwise. Seen in that light, blasphemy is just one of many acts of treason, arbitrarily and capriciously defined by those who bolster their political power with supposed religious authority.

However, we must compare this political posturing in the name of religion with the non-political heart-felt outrage of British Muslims over Rushdie's book, most of whom disapproved of implementing Khomeini's death threat in a country whose laws would thereby be violated.

Ironically, the Ayatollah's own death has put an end to *his* wish to see Salman Rushdie killed. Yet if much of the uproar over *The Satanic Verses* was staged by Khomeini to capture political headlines, much of it also can be traced directly back to sincere religious fervour. We must not forget that it all started from Bradford. Already in January 1989, Muslims in England were carrying banners saying, 'Death to Rushdie'. Nor must we overlook the fact that six Muslims died in an Islamabad protest even *before* the Ayatollah's sentence.

Moreover, Rushdie's book is not the only affront to Islam in recent months. Consider, for example, the 2,500 Chinese Muslims who in the spring of 1989 marched through Peking streets demanding the jailing of two editors for publishing a blasphemous book on Muslim sexual tendencies. Chanting, 'down with blasphemy', and 'punish China's Rushdie', Muslims and people from thirteen ethnic minorities wound their way through the streets of Peking's Moslem quarter protesting about a book called *Sex Habits*.

Presented as a compilation of essays on the sexual tastes of people around the world, the book targets Muslims with patently indecent claims. The section on Islam alleges that the purpose of a Muslim's pilgrimage to Mecca is to engage in bestiality. It further claims that the domes and towers of Islamic mosques symbolise human sexual parts. Can you imagine a statement more calculated to cast contempt on one's religious faith?

It must be emphasised that politics had nothing to do with either the source of the blasphemy or the predictable reaction of Muslims. Their religious indignation at both *Sex Habits* and *The Satanic Verses* was expressed in pamphlets which read, 'Our great and holy Islam religion has again been insulted by vicious scoundrels. Facing this kind of brazen insult, how can a true Muslim remain aloof?' How indeed! Nor were other Chinese minority groups remaining aloof from insults directed their way. In December 1988, more than three hundred banner-waving Uigur students protested against two films which took cheap shots at their particular ethnic culture. Contempt has many faces.

For a Muslim, 'remaining aloof' to blasphemy against Islam can itself be regarded as blasphemous – sometimes with deadly consequences. This fact did not escape the attention of Mr Liaqat Hussain, general secretary of Bradford's Council of Mosques: 'I don't look at moderates and extremists,' he said. 'There's only one line in Islam; you are a Moslem, all or nothing. There's no disagreement. There can't be any moderation' (*Daily Telegraph*, March 31st, 1989). 'In Islamic law,' he explained, 'libel is a criminal act. Punishment is death.'

Hussain hastened to add, 'But we cannot enforce that in Britain. We have said that from the beginning.' Perhaps so, but national boundaries did not prevent the murder of Abdullah al-Ahdal, director of the Brussels Islamic Centre, who with his deputy was killed for publicly disagreeing with Khomeini's call for the death of Mr Rushdie. So moderate was he, in fact, that he also refused to support the banning of *The Satanic Verses* in Belgium, saying, 'We live in a democratic country.'

What finally may have pulled the trigger on Mr al-Ahdal was his interview with the newspaper *la Dernière Heure* two weeks before:

> There are just a few passages in *The Satanic Verses* which can be said to blaspheme Islam . . . These did not shock me. I would not see any problem allowing the publication of this book in Belgium.

Blasphemy, no matter how slight, did not *shock* Mr al-Ahdal? Apparently to more radical Shi'ites, such indifference itself was blasphemy! That's always the case, isn't it: one man's beliefs are another man's blasphemy. That is true, even among different sects of the same religion – perhaps *especially* among different sects of the same religion!

Scepticism – The Deeper Issue

The doctrinal differences among sects within the same religion invariably trace their way back to differences in the way commonly-accepted Scriptures are viewed. There are 'liberal' and 'conservative' views of Scripture, 'progressive' and 'traditional' views. The Scriptures may be seen by some as general guidelines, or, by others, as rules to be strictly interpreted. The words of those through whom the 'revelations' have been received are seen variously as the unadulterated word of God, or of more human origin. Those who believe Scripture is unquestionably divine are likely to be the 'conservatives' holding steadfastly to traditional doctrine. Those who see Scripture as revelation mixed with human error tend to be the 'liberals' who press for more flexible application of ancient texts to current human needs.

Among Christians, there is a long (if narrow) tradition of 'higher criticism' of the Bible by sceptical scholars. Thus, for centuries, there has been free debate between 'liberals' and 'conservatives', 'traditionalists' and 'modernists'. While many of the issues are more a product of unbelieving scepticism than legitimate scholarly enquiry, other issues are indeed important. For example, of all the ancient religious texts, which books should be in the Bible? How can we be assured that the books which *are* in the Bible came from God by revelation?

Assuming those hurdles have been crossed, one must also ask, is the original text of the Bible inerrant, or does it possibly contain some mistakes? If there are mistakes, are they serious threats to revelation and doctrine, or merely inconsequential scribal hiccups? Finally, there is still the question of whether our modern translations accurately capture the meaning of the original languages in which revelation was recorded.

Despite those serious and intellectually-honest questions which one must be willing to ask, or perhaps *because* of them, the Christian faith has remained strong through the centuries. Therefore, we take it for granted that the foundations of our faith can withstand any assault, be it scholarly criticism or personal scepticism. But we must not assume that the same toleration for textual criticism is true of all religions, particularly Islam. In Islam, 'higher criticism' is both unknown and unacceptable. It is here that Salman Rushdie miscalculated. It is in this blind alley of scholarship between East and West that Rushdie found himself face-to-face with death. By entering a 'no-go' territory where the sacred is not to be questioned, he stood out as a lone silhouette on a horizon of close-mindedness, a ready target.

*

Attacking the Sacred

What Salman Rushdie did in *The Satanic Verses* was to exploit through fiction a controversial passage in the Qur'an, in order to cast doubt on the reliability of the Qur'an itself. The passage in question arises out of a confrontation between the Prophet Muhammad, who believed in the One God, and certain Arabians who believed in many gods. In a contest reminiscent of Elijah and the prophets of Baal, Muhammad asks the Arabians cynically, 'Have you seen al-Lat, al-Uzza and Manat, the third, the other?' (As if to ask, 'How can you possibly believe in these lesser deities?')

The Qur'an – thought to be direct divine revelation – further ridicules these supposed gods as 'nothing but names you have devised'. (It is worth noting, incidentally, that to the polytheistic Arabs this undoubtedly would have been blasphemy, both in content and in the ridiculing manner in which it was presented! As before, one man's faith is another man's blasphemy.)

Enter now classical Muslim commentators who suggest that in those verses Muhammad originally may have used another phrase, indicating that the pagan gods were 'exalted birds' through which the people could intercede with Allah. That would have turned the censure of pagan deities 180 degrees into their approval instead. Therefore, Muhammad quickly renounced such an interpretation of the verses, attributing such words to Satan. Hence the *Satanic* verses, from which Salman Rushdie drew the title for his book. Hence also the statement he apparently intended to make: 'Those who listen to the Devil's verses, spoken in the Devil's tongue . . . will go to the Devil in the end' (p. 484).

This, of course, is not the first time anyone has drawn such a conclusion. Islam's critics have always used these verses as evidence against the Prophet's supposed inspiration. However, Salman Rushdie is the first to capitalise on the argument through a book dripping with what seems to be a kind of contempt which arises only out of snobbish disbelief. As Rushdie himself says in the book, 'Where there is no belief, there is no blasphemy' (p. 380).

One can always wonder if a more religious scholar might have got away with pressing the point, had he couched the argument without ridicule, contempt and insensitivity. Whatever the answer, the challenge from Rushdie is clear: Muhammad could not have been the final prophet of God through whom the ultimate and final revelation of God has been given. Unfortunately for Rushdie, Islamic law is equally clear: for someone of his background to make such a challenge warrants 'dire punishment' on the Day of Judgment – and death here and now.

A Case in Point

What we must understand is that the death threat in the Rushdie affair is not unique. Death was the actual fate of another Indian writer and publisher, Raj Pal, who in the 1920s wrote a book titled *Rangeela Rasool*. Quoting extensively from Islamic books, Raj Pal dared to depict Muhammad as a womaniser. Naturally, he faced the outrage of Indian Muslims and was dragged to court. With a defence based on the authenticity of his references, Raj Pal actually won his case and was released. But that is not where the story ends.

Friday after Friday, mullahs preached sermons against Raj Pal, claiming that he was of the devil and worthy of execution. Any executioner was promised that Muhammad himself would greet him on the Day of Judgment at the door of Paradise. In response, a peasant by the name of Elmdin from Gujrat cornered Raj Pal in his office and stabbed him to death. Caught and tried for murder by the British Raj, Elmdin was given the death penalty, and he has since been regarded as a martyr.

The significance of the similarity with the Ayatollah's call for Rushdie's death did not escape the attention of the Muslim community in Britain. In October 1988, when the Bradford Muslims protested against *The Satanic Verses*, the London daily *Jang an Urdu* ran the story of Elmdin. Who would have guessed that by February of the following year Salman Rushdie would be hiding out from any 'Elmdins' intent on killing him?

Legitimate Criticism?

Not surprisingly, Salman Rushdie has protested that his book is not about criticising Islam, but rather about how people react to new ideas. In a BBC interview, Rushdie hastened from acknowledging Islam as 'one of the greatest ideas that ever came into the world' to saying, 'Let's take the themes I'm interested in and fantasise them and fabulate them and all that, so that we don't have to get into the issue: did it really happen like this or not?'

Rushdie then betrayed his apparent inner conviction by remarking: 'At the very beginning of Islam you find a conflict between the sacred text and the profane text, between revealed literature and imagined literature.' One wonders if Rushdie has been listening to the Bishop of Durham (about whom more will be said as we go along). Does he proceed with the same motives as the Bishop, who has stirred controversy by questioning the reliability and authenticity of Biblical precedents? In contrasting the two, we may be seeing a basic difference between Christianity and Islam – one permitting tolerance, one refusing it. On the other hand, tolerance of dissent has not always been a hallmark even of Christians.

In just how honourable a light can Rushdie's book be cast? David A. Kerr (*The Christian Century*, April 5th, 1989) opines that 'The book is not an objective critique of Islam, to be sure; but to protest that it is not about Islam, or at least about what Rushdie thinks of religion and revelation, is disingenuous.' Kerr notes that *The Satanic Verses* is about human *doubt*, which Rushdie calls 'the central condition of the human being in the 20th century . . . the basis of the great artistic movement known as Modernism'. Says Kerr, 'The only sense in which he admits that his book is anti-Islamic is in its attack upon an uncritical acceptance of religious authority, which has been enforced by contemporary fundamentalists.'

I could not help but notice that the issue of *The Christian Century* in which David Kerr's article is found is dominated by a front-cover picture of Dr Martin Luther King. Might Dr King have been the victim of a death threat for attacking 'an uncritical acceptance of religious authority (religiously-justified racism) . . . enforced by contemporary fundamentalists'? If, like Dr King, Rushdie were also to be killed, who would be the martyr? The condemned killer – a hero of Islam – or the one who dared challenge the religious authority of Muhammad, who, of necessity, is also viewed by believers in Jesus Christ as a spiritual counterfeit? (Have I mentioned that one man's faith is another's blasphemy?)

Somehow, the comparison between Dr Martin Luther King and Salman Rushdie seems ludicrous. The contrasting words *unselfish* and *selfish* come to mind. The causes which compelled them seem vastly distanced. One proceeded from respectful necessity; the other apparently from offensive opportunism. For one, confrontation was spelled *concern*; for the other, confrontation was spelled *contempt*. And maybe that leads us to the heart of Rushdie's blasphemy, at least as seen through non-Islamic eyes. As Martyn Harris reminds us (*Odd Man Out*, March 3rd, 1989), 'There is more devastating critique of the divine inspiration of the Koran in the *Encyclopaedia Britannica*, and nobody is burning that.'

It's not the *content* of what a serious scholar or religious critic might bring against the inspiration of the Qur'an, but the high-handed *manner* in which a disdaining intellectual unbeliever casts ridicule against the genuine faith of those who believe.

A Fully-Integrated Faith

As we explore the issues further, we shall encounter special difficulties with blasphemy, owing to the presence of an established Church in England. This rather artificial joining together of Church and state is the precarious underpinning of blasphemy laws in Britain. Yet it is important for us to remember how very different this merger of interests is from Islam's religious and political concepts. Where Britain joins the two separate interests together, in keeping with Augustinian and medieval thinking, in Islam there is no distinction between secular and spiritual authority in the first place. In England, blasphemy against the established Church and treason against the crown are each, separately, considered threats against the state. Under Islamic law, blasphemy (that is, apostasy) and treason are the same thing.

That is why, as Clifford Longley puts it, 'no purely "secular" argument, for instance in support of Rushdie's freedom of speech or Penguin Books' right to publish what they like, gains the slightest respect from a Muslim in his own terms.' For the Muslim, the secular has no claim on the sacred. In fact, the Muslim doesn't even have the word 'secular' as part of his Islamic thinking.

Blasphemy Through Islamic Eyes

This distinction here between East and West is more than academic. The average Muslim's faith is fully integrated with all other matters which we Westerners might consider to be secular. Indian-born writer Mihir Bose has put it well:

> There is a deep-seated fear of being culturally overwhelmed by the West. The culture and the religion of Islam leave no room for individualism. Even the great Moslem schisms are national and sectarian rather than theological. Organised religion for Moslems is not a matter of individual conscience and private practice (*Daily Telegraph*, February 16th, 1989).

If Westerners are comfortable with separately pigeonholing the sacred and the secular, Muslims are not. 'Islam in danger' has been the battle-cry for Muslims whenever secularism has threatened. Perhaps that is why their religion remains vibrant while ours has virtually succumbed to the onslaughts of rampant secularism. For Islam, Rushdie's book is not simply a matter of taking offence at contempt directed one's way. It represents the worst of secular thinking, which is the failure to *acknowledge* the sacred in a secular world. (Perhaps all is not lost. One of Rushdie's characters gives us this message: 'Don't think we modern types lack a spiritual dimension.')

Salman Rushdie knows where the battle lines are drawn, and he willingly has plunged much farther than any previous writer has dared to go. He has attempted to give a secular humanist vision to the birth of a great world religion, as he himself has acknowledged with remarkable boldness, if not cavalier disdain. *The Satanic Verses* displays contempt for a particular religion, but the real truth is that its author is contemptuous of *all* religion. The target of his contempt just as easily might have been the Christian religion (as demonstrated throughout the book regarding Gabriel [Gibreel] – 'What is an archangel but a puppet?' p. 460). Religion is within the realm of the sacred, and it is the realm of the sacred which Rushdie seemingly despises.

No wonder, then, that this disagreement with Islam manifests itself in characterisations beyond the limits of decency. The purely secular sets no limits on offensive human interaction. Offensive behaviour on the part of Christians and Muslims (witnessed all too often, and frequently between each other) is inconsistent with the accepted teaching of their respective religions. It has no justification. By contrast, because the secular humanist is judged by no higher authority than himself or a given identifiable majority, offensive behaviour may be expected from that quarter.

A Call For Fervour

At the end of the day, the issue is not an isolated case of blasphemy by a secular humanist who is out to vilify another's faith. Our own faith is the real issue. Again, Martyn Harris has it in sharp focus: 'Whatever we sophisticates think of it, Islam is a great world religion which gives meaning and hope to the lives of tens of millions of poor people around the world. In the West we do not take religion seriously any more, but it is a great arrogance to suggest that others should do the same.' If as Christians we fail to take our faith seriously, why should those of other faiths look to the hope that lies within us? Why should they ever be led to think that Christianity is in any way superior to Islam?

In his *Sunday Times Magazine* article on British Muslims (May 28th, 1989), Cal McCrystal quotes Dr Shabbir Akhtar, a member of the Bradford Council of Mosques, as an example of Islamic smugness in the face of Christian apathy. 'The fact that post-Enlightenment

Christians tolerate blasphemy is a matter for shame, not for pride,' says Akhtar. 'The continual blasphemies against the Christian faith have totally undermined it.' Even McCrystal's journalistic criticism of 'lapidation' (stoning to death for certain Islamic offences) was met with a response 'deploring the lapse in Christian faith'.

It's no good claiming to have a superior faith if we care so little about it that others are caused to scorn. Certainly, militancy does not always affirm the rightness of a cause, otherwise Jim Jones would have been justified for the Jonestown killings in Guyana. Yet a cause lacking fervour will convince few people of its rightness. All the more is that true when a 'Christian society' is willing to muzzle the press or ban books threatening its political security, but ignores obscene or offensive books which pose a clear and present danger to its moral and spiritual security.

Banning books, of course, is a difficult issue. There may be a need to ban revelations of military secrets which threaten national security, but the banning of other books is rarely the answer. The answer to our spiritual security lies in setting proper spiritual priorities, strengthening our personal commitment to God, and charting a course of true spiritual concern in the Church. The answer is fervour, zeal, and enthusiasm about our faith.

Today the challenge to Christian faith is great. On one flank we are faced with the rise of Islamic fundamentalism, often twisted into political terrorism, and even more often cruelly suppressive of Christian evangelism in predominantly Islamic societies. On the other flank, like conscientious Muslims themselves, we are confronted by the continuing assault of secular humanism, with its distorted contempt for anything sacred.

As Christians who believe that Jesus Christ is Lord, there is all the more reason for us to take our religion seriously. Even more reason in a Christian society, compelled by Christ's teaching of brotherly love, to demonstrate care, respect and concern for others who treasure differing religious beliefs. And even more urgency in presenting to them the good news of grace and salvation in Christ Jesus, who is the one and only true hope of the world.

As spiritual descendants of Abraham we who are Christians can, along with Muslims, claim Abraham as our father. The question we must ask lovingly of Muslims, however, is: Who is our *mother*? Is it Hagar the slave woman, who represents the futility of legalistic worship, or Sarah the free woman, who represents the spiritual freedom we have in Jesus Christ? The Apostle Paul tells us in Galatians 4:21–5:1 that 'Hagar stands for Mount Sinai in Arabia and corresponds to the present city of Jerusalem, because she is in slavery with her children. But the Jerusalem that is above is free, and she is our mother.'

Beyond the controversy over *The Satanic Verses*, and beyond the issue of whether Muhammad is God's final prophet, it's a higher view of God to which Christ calls us, whether Muslim or Christian. 'We are not children of the slave woman, but of the free woman. It is for freedom that Christ has set us free.' Enough of empty prayer-book ritual among nominal Christians! Enough of legalistic rule-keeping among even fervent Muslims! For in Christ (Galatians 5:6), 'The only thing that counts is faith expressing itself through love.'

As Christians, we must let our faith express itself in love to all people, who, like us, are made in God's image. Through Christian love, we can share with those who seek salvation the release from fear and the peace of mind which come through obedient submission to Christ.

3

Just What Is Blasphemy?

In Search of a Useful Definition

> That in the captain's but a choleric word,
> Which in the soldier is flat blasphemy.
>
> William Shakespeare
> *Measure for Measure*

In its June 1976 issue of *Gay News*, a homosexual-run newspaper, the publishers printed a poem by a Professor James Kirkup entitled 'The Love that Dares to Speak its Name'. Accompanying it was an illustrated drawing of its content. The poem describes in explicit detail supposed acts of illicit sex with the body of Christ following his crucifixion, and also suggests that during his lifetime Jesus engaged in promiscuous homosexual practices with his chosen Apostles and others.

Upon private prosecution by Mrs Mary Whitehouse, the editor and publishers of *Gay News* were brought to trial and convicted of blasphemous libel. For his part as editor and majority shareholder, Denis Lemon was sentenced to nine months' imprisonment (suspended for eighteen months) and fined £500. Gay News Ltd were fined £1,000. After the Court of Appeal affirmed the decision of the lower court (except for quashing the sentence of imprisonment as being not 'appropriate'), the appellants were granted further appeal to the House of Lords. In the House, the convictions were upheld.

The first case of its kind to be prosecuted in fifty-five years, *Whitehouse v. Gay News Ltd and Lemon* was historic in the field of blasphemy libel. Charged as an offence against the Christian religion, there was little question regarding the jury's verdict. As Viscount Dilhorne noted, 'That finding has not been challenged in this appeal, nor could it have been with the slightest prospect of success.' The only issue before the House of Lords was the intent required for the crime of blasphemy.

However, the act of blasphemy itself has not always been so easily defined or applied to a given case. Moreover, the definition of the offence has gone through a major shift in emphasis over the centuries. Initially, blasphemy looked more like heresy – the Christian equivalent to Islàm's apostasy. It included any matter which contradicted the teaching of the Church of England or tended to undermine its authority. You can easily see its parallel in the crime of sedition, which was any matter likely to undermine the authority of the king. Now, however, the focus of the crime has shifted to the *manner* of one's communication rather than the *content* of the matter itself. A quick review of the cases will set the scene.

Blasphemy in Review

During the eighteenth and early nineteenth centuries, any number of religious writings were suppressed as blasphemous. Woolston, a Cambridge don, was jailed for denying Biblically-recorded miracles. He was joined in prosecution by a host of Unitarians, Deists and others. Depending on who is counting, anywhere from dozens to several hundred people were jailed in the row over Thomas Paine's *Age of Reason*.

All this was possible because at common law it was a misdemeanour to publish any matter which denied the truth of the Christian religion, the Bible, the Book of Common Prayer, or the existence of God. In his *Digest of the Criminal Law*, Mr Stephen explained why no more was needed for blasphemy: 'The cases all proceed upon the plain principle that the public importance of the Christian religion is so great that no one is allowed to deny its truth.'

Mr Justice Alderson, in the *Gathercole* case (1838), added an interesting twist to the proposition. He reckoned that, since only the established Church is part of the constitution, an attack on other religions would not 'shake the fabric of society', a formula approved by other justices. However, such a notion of this 'Christian offence' raises some compelling questions.

For example, was the fabric of a modern Christian society shaken by the appearance of a disgusting poem in a limited-readership homosexual newspaper? When Mary Whitehouse initiated the prosecution in the *Gay News* case, was she any less the object of embarrassment to many 'liberal' Christians than the object of sneering by homosexuals? Did fifty thousand British Christians march in protest against *The Last Temptation of Christ*, as fifty thousand Muslims (very much a part of today's societal fabric) marched against *The Satanic Verses*? What is more likely to 'shake the fabric of Christian society' than a bishop of the Church of England who announces on Easter weekend that he doesn't believe in the bodily resurrection of Christ? Such a test of blasphemy (shaking the fabric of society) hardly served the nation then, and may well point the finger of blame at the wrong targets now.

Three early cases illustrate the initial shift away from heresy's being regarded as blasphemy. *Rex v. Hetherington* (1841), for example, saw Lord Denman direct the jury:

> Gentlemen, the question is not altogether a matter of [one's] opinion, but that it must be, in a great degree, a question as to the tone and style, and spirit, in which such inquiries are conducted. Because, a difference of opinion may subsist not only as between different sects of Christians but also with regard to the great doctrines of Christianity itself . . . but, if they be carried on in a sober and temperate and decent style, even those discussions may be tolerated.

In *Shore v. Wilson* (1842), Mr Justice Erskine agreed: 'It is indeed still blasphemy, punishable at common law, scoffingly or irreverently to ridicule or impugn the doctrines of the Christian faith . . . yet a man may . . . soberly and reverently examine and question the truth of those doctrines which have been assumed as essential to it.'

In perhaps the most significant movement away from *content* as blasphemy to *manner* as blasphemy, the 1883 case of *Rex v. Foote* reacted to a cartoon in the *Freethinker* depicting God's posterior, wearing huge checked trousers, as illustrating Exodus 33:22–3, 'When my glory passes by, I will put you in a cleft in the rock and cover you with my hand until I have passed by. Then I will remove my hand and you will see my back . . .' Here, Mr Justice North defined blasphemy as 'a contumelious [insulting] reproach or profane scoffing against the Christian religion or the Holy Scriptures, or exposing Scripture or Christianity to ridicule, contempt or derision'.

Lord Coleridge moved even closer to abandoning the former blasphemy-by-heresy in directing the jury in *Rex*

Just What Is Blasphemy?

v. Ramsey and Foote that 'mere denial of the truths of Christianity does *not* amount to blasphemy, but only a wilful intention to pervert, insult, and mislead others by means of licentious and contumelious abuse applied to sacred subjects'. Lord Coleridge set a new tone for blasphemy when he ruled that, if the decencies of controversy were observed, even fundamentals of religion might be attacked.

Before we struggle further with the definition of blasphemy, then, it is important to distinguish carefully *heresy*, which was formerly an ecclesiastical offence and now no longer applies to anyone other than the clergy (and, in practice, not even to them). Punishable by death prior to 1677, heresy is punishable currently by excommunication or censure. Unlike blasphemy, which deals with the manner in which an opposing belief might be stated, heresy deals with the holding of an opinion repugnant to a doctrine which is either essential or very important to the Christian faith. Once again, the final arbiter of the offended doctrine is the established Church.

As Paley, the great orator and defender of the faith, has observed, 'Christianity is but ill defended by refusing audience or toleration to the objection of unbelievers.' Put heavy emphasis here on the word *unbelievers*. Whereas a challenge to faith by unbelievers no longer falls within the ambit of blasphemy laws, Church leaders do not yet have complete rein when disagreeing on issues of doctrine. A long lead, perhaps, but not complete rein. More on that later.

This legal shift away from heresy-as-blasphemy must have brought a sigh of relief to all nonconformists, atheists, and other critics of the established Church. To bring the point even closer to home, the very words you are reading in this book – which are sometimes critical of the established Church and of a lagging Christian society – easily could have violated the blasphemy laws little more than a century ago. As you might guess, then, I do not take lightly the potential for abuse which can inhere in such laws.

Emphasising the Manner

It is of the utmost significance, therefore, that the crime of blasphemy eventually was limited to any vilifying attack on Christianity which was likely to 'outrage the feelings of believers', or the 'general body of the community'. Instead of being used offensively against enemies of the Church, the blasphemy law became a defensive weapon against injury to the feelings of Christians. Even so, one wonders if hurt feeling in the hearts of British Christians was the central concern in cases brought after that time.

Take the case of *Rex v. Gott*, for example. In this 1920s' case, J.W. Gott, a Freethinker, published and sold on the streets a pamphlet called *Ribticklers, or Questions for Parsons*. Apparently it was a response in kind to an evangelical tract called *Questions for Infidels*. Gott's blasphemy was a series of corny jokes like: 'Is it true that much of the Bible reads as if it had been written in a pub under the influence of spirits?' For this marginal attempt at humour, Gott was prosecuted five times and imprisoned three times, once with nine months of hard labour.

If *manner* is to be the test, the questionable use of humour in taking issue with the Christian religion could put one at risk of prosecution for blasphemy. Yet one can only speculate how many times a week comedians take pot shots at the Church, Christianity, and faith in general without the slightest murmur of complaint from their audiences. Has even *manner* reached such levels of tolerance (apathy?) that blasphemy is no longer an issue relevant to our time?

*

Just What Is Blasphemy?

Breaching the Peace

A slightly different tack taken in some of the cases assumes perhaps more than one safely *can* assume in today's climate of religious indifference: the possibility that blasphemous words might, in fact, have a riotous effect upon society. Perhaps there was a time when religious dissent or contemptuous ridicule amounted to 'fighting words', but the rarity of cases alone (five between 1883 and 1922, and only one since) would suggest that breach of the peace over religious issues is hardly likely.

Lord Sumner, in *Bowman v. Secular Society Ltd* (1917) argued that irreligious words are basically a matter between the Creator and the man who uses them. All that secular courts can do is to ensure that irreligious words don't bring about specific harm to society, be it endangering the peace, depraving public morality generally, or shaking the very fabric of society. In *Bowman*, the court held that a company formed to promote the secularisation of the state was not unlawful, although one of its objects was to deny Christianity. If their goals were offensive, their manner of presenting their agenda was not.

Lord Sumner himself, however, recognised that such a definition of blasphemy would flutter in the capricious breezes of public opinion about religion:

> The words, as well as the acts, which tend to endanger society differ from time to time in proportion as society is stable or insecure in fact, or is believed by its reasonable members to be open to assault. In the present day, meetings or processions are held lawful which a hundred and fifty years ago would have been deemed seditious, and this is not because the law is weaker or has changed, but, because the times have changed, society is stronger than before. In the

present day, reasonable men do not apprehend the dissolution or the downfall of society because religion is publicly assailed by methods not scandalous.

If potential for breach of the peace is to be the test of blasphemy, then two points immediately come to mind. The first is a preview of yet another issue – whether the blasphemy laws ought to be extended to cover contempt against non-Christian faiths. For the truth of the matter is that, since the early 1900s when this case was decided, the only breach of the peace in the face of religious blasphemy in this country has come from the sometimes-violent Muslim demonstrations in protest against *The Satanic Verses*. On that basis alone, Rushdie's book could have been declared blasphemous. If breach of the peace is not to be a *required element* of proving blasphemy, it certainly stands as strong *evidence* that the limits of decent controversy have been exceeded.

The second point is that Lord Sumner was right about changing times. Indeed times have changed so significantly that few Christians these days would take to the streets in protest at scurrilous remarks directed against Christianity, no matter how inflammatory. It reminds me of the prohibition of the US Constitution against 'cruel and unusual punishment' and the death penalty debate. The courts have allowed so few instances of capital punishment in the United States over the past two decades that the death penalty has indeed become *unusual*. Because, then, it *is* unusual, the argument is made that it is therefore unconstitutional. A self-implementing circuit of logic, if you will.

Similarly, the blasphemer's time has come! Allow blasphemy to go unchallenged long enough, and there will come a time when it is seen no longer as blasphemy! The breach-of-the-peace approach to defining blasphemy should threaten no one today. There is little likelihood of *any* public outcry, much less breach of the public peace. We've come a long way from book burning, heresy hangings and parliamentary protests. Perhaps too far. Perhaps the pendulum has swung to the opposite extreme. If *intolerance* was born out of religious zeal, *indifference* has been born out of religious tolerance.

Searching for the Essence

This takes us full circle back to the rationale for the most recent blasphemy case, *Whitehouse v. Gay News and Lemon*. Although Lord Scarman quoted with approval the breach-of-peace definition given by Lord Sumner in *Bowman*, he limits the *actus reus* of the crime (that is, the acts which must be proved) to the blasphemous words themselves, wholly apart from either the person's intent or the potential effect the words might have on society:

> Every publication is said to be blasphemous which contains any contemptuous, reviling, scurrilous or ludicrous matter relating to God, Jesus Christ, or the Bible, or the formularies of the Church of England as by law established.

Therefore, what we are looking for in blasphemy today is anything which insults, offends, or vilifies the Deity, or Christ, or the Christian religion as interpreted by the Church of England – whether or not a riot is likely to break out as a result.

If contemptuous language related to things sacred is offensive without regard to potential for breach of the peace, what is the controlling rationale for blasphemy laws? Mr Justice Erskine suggested at least one possibility: 'Sober argument you may answer, but indecent reviling you cannot, and therefore the law steps in and punishes it.' Is that why *Gay News* was prosecuted – because we couldn't answer an argument about whether Jesus was a homosexual? Is this the reason Mr Gott was sentenced to hard labour – because the Church had no way to respond to his implication that the Scriptures were written by a bunch of drunks?

I suggest that we have missed the point of blasphemy when we reduce it to *unanswerable* ridicule. The person who is reviling our faith is not looking for answers! He doesn't care at all about dialogue, meaningful or not. Are we to believe that Salman Rushdie really intended *The Satanic Verses* as a vehicle for serious dialogue with Muslims as to the genuineness of Muhammad's revelations?

Venting Inner Rage

Blasphemy laws are not designed to keep gentlemanly discussion of religious issues from deteriorating into frenzied mud-slinging. Blasphemy laws recognise what blasphemy produces: gut-level *outrage*! It is that welling up of the emotions that makes a peaceful person want to throttle somebody. It's the feeling that one gets when his house is broken into or his car is stolen. It's that overwhelming sense of rage you would feel if you saw someone intentionally knock down a helpless old woman, or were to hear that your daughter had been raped. It is *justifiable anger*. It is *righteous indignation*. It is what happens when your most serious psychological nerves have been touched.

But *why* the anger, *why* the indignation, *why* the shock? It is because bedrock values have been turned on their heads. The bounds of human decency have been crossed. The demands of reason have been unmet. It is like a parent who is so incensed that he or she cannot give the child a reason for a negative response. It is too obvious for words! In an ideal world, blasphemy laws

Just What Is Blasphemy?

take account of the impulses which rush adrenaline-like through our personal value systems when sacred values have been turned front to back.

I remember having such feelings when the Los Angeles television news broadcast I was watching showed scenes from a local Christmas parade. Among the gaily decorated floats passing by before thousands of California families, and millions more on television, was one that was *gayly* decorated – by an organisation of homosexuals pressing a case for gay rights. My immediate impulse was to rush to the scene and burn the float! Normally a passive, turn-the-other-cheek kind of individual, I was outraged by this intentional affront to decency. It made me want to do something I normally never should have considered. It tempted me to breach the peace!

You'll be relieved to know that, instead of following my impulses, I vented my feelings by writing a more soberly-considered article for the *Los Angeles Times*. Thankfully, it was a far more reasoned expression of dissent, and actually achieved some very positive results.

Given a religiously-cohesive society, blasphemy laws make a statement about the importance which society places upon values. They bolster the collective conscience. They channel the outrage. They enforce the offence, substituting the power of the state for the temptation to individual violence where there is nowhere else to turn for appropriate redress. To that extent they lessen any potential for breach of the peace.

Even if violent reaction is not likely in a spiritually-lethargic society, and even if there is no more than a rare call for prosecution under the statutes, blasphemy laws can set a tone reflective of decency. Even the non-religious person can appreciate blasphemy laws on the basis that they help protect religion as a cultural value supportive of societal harmony. In the latter part of the book we shall develop more fully the need for a sense of the sacred – whether that be in a strictly religious context or otherwise.

Suffice it to say at this point, it is not out of place in a pluralistic society to have blasphemy laws which educate and elevate. Laws which create certain social expectations, to the betterment of society at large, whether Christian, non-Christian, or even non- religious.

Blasphemy laws, therefore, may well serve a variety of laudable purposes: to protect respected institutions and their doctrines; to guard against insult to individual religious feelings; to maintain public order; and to uphold religion as a cultural value to the whole of society. Yet that may not be the end of the story. In Britain, certainly, it is *not* the end of the story.

4

Can Non-Christians Be Ignored?

Equal Protection in a Pluralistic Society

> When I mention religion I mean the Christian religion; and not only the Christian religion, but the Protestant religion; and not only the Protestant religion, but the Church of England.
>
> Henry Fielding
> *Tom Jones* (Parson Thwackum)

Having said that blasphemy laws can provide a valuable service to society, it remains to be seen whether in a pluralistic society such blasphemy laws ought to be either extended to other religions or abolished altogether. One can hardly deny that people of all faiths can experience the outrage that blasphemy produces. After all, as Lord Sumner reminds us, 'to insult a Jew's religion is not less likely to promote a fight than to insult an Episcopalian's'. Therefore, limiting protection for such outrage only to Christians, or, worse yet, only to the established Church, is no longer justifiable.

Ours is not a religiously-cohesive society. No longer

can it safely be said that the Church of England is the state Church, other than in name and formality. In terms of active participation, the established Church does not represent anywhere near a majority of British citizens. (Out of fifty-two million citizens, only twenty-seven million are christened by the Church).

Speaking even more broadly of the Christian religion, the words of Chief Justice Hale in *Rex v. Taylor* (1676) have a hollow ring in 1989: 'Christianity is part and parcel of the laws of England; and therefore to reproach the Christian religion is to speak in subversion of the law.'

More true to our times is the frankness with which Lord Scarman spoke in the *Gay News* case:

> I do not subscribe to the view that the common law offence of blasphemous libel serves no useful purpose in the modern law. On the contrary, I think there is a case for legislation extending it to protect the religious beliefs and feelings of non-Christians. The offence belongs to a group of criminal offences designed to safeguard the internal tranquillity of the kingdom. In an increasingly plural society such as that of modern Britain, it is necessary not only to respect the differing religious beliefs, feelings, and practices of all but also to protect them from scurrility, vilification, ridicule, and contempt.

Today, of course, Muslims are calling for the extension of blasphemy laws to cover insults against Islam. Mr Abdal Choudhary, convener of the British Moslem Action Front, has argued before the courts that in 1883, when the British Empire extended to colonies throughout the world, including India, it had been established that blasphemy laws extended beyond Christianity to 'sacred presence or objects', which would cover other religions.

The government, so far, have responded coolly, maintaining that historic Church-state ties prevent such a move. Naturally, that argument is as frail as the dwindling threads which bind Church and state together in a pluralistic and ever-more-secular society which often pays little more than lip-service to the Christian faith.

Interestingly, not all religious minorities desire an extension of the blasphemy laws. Chief Rabbi Jakobovits, for example, believes Britain already has sufficient protection in a package of legislation including laws on pornography, libel, incitement of racial hatred, subversion, and breaches of national security. The Chief Rabbi is certain that extension of the blasphemy laws is not the answer:

> In my view, Jews should not seek an extension of the blasphemy laws. In any event, the Jewish definition of blasphemy is confined to 'cursing God' and does not include an affront to any prophet (not even Moses, in our case). Living in a predominantly Christian society, with an established Church, we should be quite content to leave the legislation on blasphemy as it stands, enshrining the national respect for the majority faith.

Naturally, not all Jews in Britain might agree with the Chief Rabbi. Undoubtedly, many Jews would prefer that the blasphemy laws be abolished altogether.

In his thoughtful letter to *The Times* (March 1st, 1989), Dr John Habgood, the Archbishop of York, reminds us of the risk we run when we contemplate opening the Pandora's box of blasphemy laws:

> Religion is a luxuriant growth. Alongside major historical traditions is a tangled mass of lesser and newer ones, not always easily identifiable, fiercely

competitive, some of them much given to litigation, and with beliefs which range from the profoundly impressive to the suspiciously barmy.

Where does one draw the line? Is Ron Hubbard, for instance, a candidate for posthumous inviolability?

The Archbishop's own test? Forget 'the degree of offence felt by individuals', he suggests. Concentrate instead on 'the place within society of the religious body in question, this to include such factors as extensiveness, public commitment, and common concern with other religious bodies for social stability'. By this test, presumably, all major religions would fall within the law's protection, and a jury composed of unbiased men and women could fairly and reasonably sort out all other claimants.

Clifford Longley is not so sure. In his *Times* column (February 25th, 1989), he thinks blasphemy is too complex for simple solutions:

> Even if the law of blasphemy were to be expanded to cover non-Christian religions, it is hard to imagine an English jury convicting Salman Rushdie for his *Satanic Verses*. It is too subtle and theological an assault to expect a jury of passengers on the Clapham omnibus to take the true measure of it. Blasphemy is a very slippery concept.

Really? To say that a largely 'Christian society' might not rise up in the face of blasphemy directed its own way is not to suggest that the general public from which jurors are drawn could not appreciate the insult to Islam contained in Rushdie's book. I have tried some fairly complicated and subtle cases before ordinary jurors and I've never found them lacking. In fact, the common person in the jury box often understands the subtleties of human nature even better than we professionals, who rarely deign to rub elbows with those who daily ride the Clapham omnibus.

On the other hand, I am not unsympathetic to Longley's proposal that blasphemy be reshaped as an action in libel, covering as it does the impugning of one's character. All that need be done, he suggests, is to open the libel laws to actions brought on behalf of 'revered founders of major religions' as if they were still alive today, as indeed they are in the minds of their followers. In one clean move, Longley suggests, this would both avoid the abstract and often subjective nature of blasphemy laws and also extend protection to the founders of non-Christian religions. I hasten to point out, however, that some major religions have no 'founder' whatever – notably Hinduism, Shintoism and Taoism.

What, too, if the contempt is levelled against *God*? Longley, in somewhat of an aside, suggested that 'God is above being insulted'. That may be true in the sense that pettiness is inconsistent with God's character. It may also be true in the sense that Jesus himself opened up the possibility that even a blasphemer could be forgiven (Matt. 12:22). Yet it was *God* who first commanded that his name should not be reviled (Lev. 24:15–16). God himself legislated the first blasphemy law! If there is some way in which he is above insult, make no mistake about it: God *cares* (for our own sakes as well as his) about how we treat his character and reputation.

Furthermore, suppose some vilifying contempt is levelled at some revered doctrine, or at a given religion in general without reference to any recognised founder? In such a case, the laws of libel would be of no value. Nor would any other current law be available to prevent the contempt or redress the wrong.

There is yet another relevant factor to be considered regarding libel, brought to our attention recently by bold headlines. In the wake of record libel damages and the case of *Private Eye* v. *Sonia Sutcliffe*, estranged wife of the Yorkshire Ripper, one can only wonder what libel damages would be appropriate for impugning the character of Joseph Smith, Ellen G. White, Buddha, Muhammad, or – imagine it – *God*! Who would be so bold as to collect (and spend) the damages on their behalf? Longley is right, of course, in suggesting a fine (where the money goes to the state) and confiscation of the offensive material.

For lawyers, I'm afraid, this approach has as many headaches as blasphemy laws themselves. Longley's proposal takes what is essentially a private cause of action and makes it a public claim – certainly not unheard of, but not the easy solution it superficially appears to be. Permitting private prosecution of a criminal libel charge does not equate easily with public prosecution of what historically is a personal civil action.

Nor, I suggest, does it capture the essence of the cause of action. At stake is not simply the impugning of one's character, even the character of Jesus, Muhammad, or Buddha. At stake is a broader respect for that which is held to be sacred.

A Question of Intent

If it were agreed that the laws of blasphemy ought to be extended to non-Christian religions, what acts should be prohibited? Perhaps it would be some variation of the following formula: every publication is said to be blasphemous which contains any contemptuous, reviling, or scurrilous matter relating to the Deity, persons or things which are objects of faith or devotion, or teachings held essential or important to a given religion. It is not blasphemous to speak or publish opinions hostile to any religion if the publication is couched in decent and temperate language. The test to be applied is as to the *manner* in which beliefs are

Can Non-Christians Be Ignored?

advocated or statements are made, and not as to their *substance*.

However, if we felt comfortable with such a formula as descriptive of the *act* of blasphemy, we have yet to decide the *mens rea* of the crime (that is, the mental element which must be proved). If you will excuse momentarily the fussiness of a criminal law professor, I am obliged to point out that every *true* crime *must* have a mental element. All the more remarkable, therefore, is the decision of the House of Lords in the *Gay News* case. As the law stands, guilt of the offence of blasphemy does not depend on the accused's having an intent to blaspheme. It is sufficient for the prosecution to prove (a) that the *publication* was intentional and (b) that the matter published was in fact blasphemous. By the Law Lords' ruling, a person need not even know that the words would, or might have, the effect of shock or insult!

Although the majority ruling denied it, it is difficult to conclude that blasphemy is now anything other than a crime of *strict liability* – that is, without any intent requirement whatsoever. The House of Lords were correct, of course, to reject any requirement of a *specific* intent to blaspheme. It should not be necessary to show that someone set out purposely to effectuate a blasphemy, wilfully to offend someone, or to bring contempt upon some group of believers. *Specific intent* requirements, typically, are reserved for crimes serious enough to merit imprisonment.

On the other hand, eliminating the element of intent altogether from a charge of blasphemy comes close to being blasphemy against accepted *legal* principles! Strict liability offences form an exclusive, carefully-limited set of criminal offences. Typically, we regard traffic offences and parking tickets as holding the offender strictly liable. You say you have a good excuse for not returning to the parking meter before the time expired? Sorry, we don't want to hear about it! Given just the right excuse, of course, the judge might show mercy. However, the offender is not legally entitled to defend against a proven prohibited act.

Where there is an overriding public policy of great importance, other violations might also be tagged as strict liability offences. For example, the serving of alcohol to under-age minors is one such offence. It doesn't matter if a genuine-looking form of identification indicated the customer was of legal age, nor that he had grey hair and the wrinkles of a ninety-year-old. If it turns out that he is under the legal age, the bartender is guilty of an offence. Full stop! The safety valve for such 'civil offences' disguised as crimes is that no imprisonment is permitted and only moderate fines are imposed. The idea is to use the criminal laws as a means of administrative control.

By contrast, where the charge is as serious as blasphemy – entailing as it does its own threat to the character of the accused, if convicted – then *some* intent ought to be required as an element of the offence. Otherwise, we too risk creating a 'chilling effect' on free speech. For example, booksellers like W.H. Smith or Waterstone, with thousands of book titles on their shelves, would be burdened with reviewing each of those books for any possible blasphemy which might be contained in them. With the risk of being guilty under the law if they should overlook some offensive material, few booksellers would keep open their doors. Naturally, without booksellers the free flow of ideas would be brought to a standstill.

There must be either a knowing intent to publish the offensive matter, or a communication of the blasphemy through gross negligence, or a wilful and wanton disregard for the risk of its being communicated. In some way, there must be actual or imputed awareness of the offensive nature of the publication and of the fact that it is being published.

I think Smith and Hogan, in their commentary (p. 686) on the *Gay News* case, have just about got it right: 'Presumably it must be shown that the defendant was aware of the presence and understood the meaning of the offending words. If they were in a foreign language and he believed they were a recipe for Christmas pudding, he would surely not be guilty.' Hear, hear!

It reminds one of the widely-distributed publicity for Billy Graham's recent British campaign, aimed at attracting the public's curiosity to a man who could provide them with life's answers. The advertising signs, reading 'FELI, IFEL, LIFE', unwittingly contained a Hindu obscenity!

In a society honouring free speech, the importance of the mental element cannot be overstated. A defence must be available to the accused whenever there is doubt. This should in no way jeopardise any prosecution for blasphemy. In the *Gay News* case, for instance, it can hardly be argued that the editor of the *Gay News* was unaware of the nature of the matter deemed to be blasphemous, or, less yet, that he did not intend to publish it. What may be clouding the issue is whether the accused must have had a *specific* intent to blaspheme, and of course that is not required. A drunk driver need not intend to kill his victim. It is enough that he decides to drive, aware of his intoxicated condition, and thus the risk that he might kill someone. Likewise, with blasphemy it is enough that one proceeds with publication, aware of the risk that it crosses the line of acceptable communication.

Toward Equal Protection

Whatever specific form future legislation or court rulings might take, I should think it elementary that the blasphemy laws of Britain can no longer be limited to the

Christian religion, much less to any special ties with the Church of England. Because blasphemy is a common-law offence, there would appear to be no difficulty in extending it to religions other than Christianity, apart from the reluctance of the judges to widen the scope of common-law offences.

The important point is that, in a pluralistic society, we differ – sometimes vehemently – in our understanding of God and how, and through whom, we are to relate to him. Yet although we may differ, we must join hands with people of faith in every religion who take the idea of sacredness seriously. On that front, if on no other, we can stand united as one.

5

Second Thoughts About Blasphemy

Might Blasphemy Laws Fall Into the Wrong Hands?

> Love your neighbour, yet pull not down your hedge.
>
> George Herbert
> *Jacula Prudentium*

The law professor in me has been trying to get out for the past several pages. Perhaps more in American law schools than in traditional British legal training, we rely heavily on the use of what we call the Socratic method of teaching. The truth is that Socrates probably would take another draught of hemlock if he knew his name was being lent to our particular style of teaching, but the idea is at least marginally similar. In our Socratic method, we regularly employ the use of hypotheticals in order to test the students' understanding of legal theory or to evaluate a given rule of law or particular piece of legislation. Perhaps we could benefit from a little Socratic dialogue regarding blasphemy.

As a means of testing the various considerations of the previous chapter, let's use our proposed new blasphemy statute, to cover non-Christian religions. (Inclusion of the word 'knowingly' would require proof of a general criminal intent.)

> Every publication is said to be blasphemous which knowingly contains any contemptuous, reviling, or scurrilous matter relating to the Deity, persons or things which are objects of faith or devotion, or teachings held essential or important to a given religion.
> It is not blasphemous to speak or publish opinions hostile to any religion if the publication is couched in decent and temperate language.
> The test to be applied is as to the manner in which beliefs are advocated or statements are made, and not as to their substance.

If Parliament amended Britain's blasphemy laws accordingly, or if the courts modified the common-law offence as they have a right to do, we might be surprised at the directions in which just a few hypotheticals could take us. We can assume that sincerity of belief or rightness of motive is not a defence to the crime of blasphemy. The only issue is whether the statements cross the line from being respectful religious discussion to vilifying another's faith.

Hypothesis 1: Are Blasphemy and Heresy Distinguishable?

Suppose a Christian speaker or author were to contend, in the most respectful manner possible, that Muhammad was not a true prophet of God, that the Qur'an is not a revelation of God, and that the Five Pillars (Islamic acts of obedience) are merely human tradition. Could Muslims press a prosecution for blasphemy on the basis that he was contemptuous of Islam? Should

Second Thoughts About Blasphemy

we all agree that the expressed opinion, though hostile to Islam, was not stated in a hostile *manner* and therefore falls outside the scope of blasphemy?

As are many law-school hypotheticals, this one is drawn from real life. Christians in India and Pakistan used to write such books, respectfully and without hostility, but since 1960 those books have largely disappeared. If in England the idea of blasphemy is the absence of *civility*, in a predominantly Muslim country such writings can be the object of prosecution, *regardless* of their respectful civility.

If we now alter the hypothetical, we can find ourselves in radically different territory. Suppose the speaker or author were to say without any apparent rancour that Muhammad was a *liar* by claiming to be a chosen prophet of God and by convincing others that the 'revelations' in the Qur'an were from God. Have we now crossed the boundary of fair comment?

The problem, naturally, comes in the way the statement is couched. The first statement – a denial of the central teachings of Islam – indirectly *implies* that Muhammad must not have been telling the truth to his followers, whereas the second statement forthrightly uses a word – 'liar' – which is almost universally emotive, if not contemptuous. Instead of giving Muhammad *some* benefit of the doubt (perhaps he was misguided), we now have a direct accusation of bad character (he was a deceiver).

Of course, the opposite case would also apply. The Muslim who rejects Jesus as a human revelation of God, in the face of Jesus's own claims of being God in the flesh, is implying – at least from a Christian perspective – that Jesus was not telling the truth. In that regard, he correctly could use the word 'liar' to underscore his honest belief about Jesus.

In fact, the issue is more complicated than that, because Muslims claim that it is *Christians* who have exalted Jesus to a degree of divinity. Believing that Jesus never claimed to be God, Muslims believe that it is not Jesus but *Christians* who are liars. Yet the issue remains: Is it possible to escalate from *content* to *manner* merely by how we choose to couch what in essence may be the same assertion?

In making these distinctions, we are not speaking as hypothetically as it might seem. Part of the charge of blasphemy against Salman Rushdie is his implication in *The Satanic Verses* that the Qur'an is not of divine origin. Are dozens of Christian books which take the same viewpoint any less blasphemous? If so, is it because they do not fictionally associate Muhammad's wives with prostitutes or attribute Muhammad with a name meant for the devil? Is *politeness* the antidote to blasphemy? Is a *lack* of politeness or civility the essence of blasphemy legislation? If so, who is to determine issues of politeness? The jury, of course. However, that raises yet another interesting possibility.

It is altogether possible that a given British courtroom could be dominated by Muslims, both as judge and jury. If that should occur, do we run the risk that, despite the disclaimers given in the suggested formulation, Muslim judges and juries would feel compelled by their religious beliefs to decide that any heresy against Islam is automatically contemptuous language?

On the other side of the coin, suppose we have a *non*-Muslim jury presented with undeniable proof of heresy against the teaching of Muhammad or the Qur'an. Will Muslims cry foul when unquestionable blasphemy in the eyes of Islam is held by an unappreciative jury to be non-blasphemous?

Not An Exclusively Muslim Difficulty

Lest recent events cause us to focus too narrowly on the possible actions of Muslims, we must not forget

Second Thoughts About Blasphemy

that there are other, sometimes uncannily similar, religions to consider. Anyone who walks north on London's Exhibition Road past the Victoria and Albert Museum is likely to be engaged in religious discussion by some awfully good people whose appearances, being far from Muslim-like, would give no warning that major theological differences were afoot. I refer, of course, to the Mormons who practise sidewalk evangelism outside the Visitors Center for the Church of Jesus Christ of Latter Day Saints.

The words 'Latter Day' give us our first clue to the similarity between Muslims and Mormons. Both believe in a prophet of God coming centuries after Jesus (Joseph Smith, in the case of the Mormons), and both believe that they possess God's final revelation, which for Mormons is the Book of Mormon. Each faith pays homage to Jesus as a great prophet of God, but each denies the exclusivity and finality of his Lordship. Each religion stresses strict moral codes and exercises stringent discipline of wayward members (certainly, for Mormons, not including death). Even a history of polygamy is shared by these two religions (although no longer officially sanctioned by Mormons).

Curiously, among the many attacks claiming the Book of Mormon to be a spurious document have been allegations, not unlike *The Satanic Verses*, that highlight the human aspects of its origin. Any number of 'Salman Rushdies' have written non-fiction books containing scathing attacks on Joseph Smith, castigating both his personal character and his supposed revelations. Recent changes in Church teaching have also called into question the whole idea of 'latter day' revelation. For example, where blacks were once denied equal status in the Mormon faith, pursuant to a relatively recent 'revelation' official church teaching has now broken down racial barriers. Naturally, detractors of the faith have had a field day with the timing of the 'revelation' and what is seen to be a convenient response to growing external pressures. (As Muhammad's wife says in *The Satanic Verses*, 'Your God certainly jumps to it when you need him to fix things up for you' p. 386.)

So we are faced once again with what to do about a book which 'exposes' as fraudulent the very basic foundations of another's faith. Can any degree of politeness and respect keep it from being blasphemous to those who share that faith? Just how hard hitting can a critic be before receiving his summons to court? In an increasingly rights-conscious and litigious society, one wonders if renewed attention given to blasphemy laws (particularly if expanded) might not bring a spate of complaints from the adherents of competing religions.

Hypothesis 2: Lost in the Translation

Suppose a rather deranged individual were to stand on the public pavement across from Canterbury Cathedral, carrying a placard bearing the words: 'Jesus is a bastard; his mother was a whore.' I throw in the word 'deranged' for we lawyers, who need to keep thinking about whether blasphemy is a strict liability offence. If so, a person with diminished mental capacity presumably might still be guilty of violating the law. That issue aside, however, is anyone prepared to deny that the words constitute blasphemy?

American judges in the case of *New York* v. *Ruggles* (1811), from which the hypothetical is taken, certainly were not prepared to exclude it as blasphemous. Nor were they interested in the argument that blasphemy is not possible in a country where there is a separation between Church and state.

Beyond that, I am intrigued about the nature of the words used in the *Ruggles* case, and about a curious tie-in with Islamic teaching. From the perspective of

Second Thoughts About Blasphemy   67

Muslims, we Christians go about daily impugning God's purity by claiming that Jesus is his son. They believe that we are talking about 'son' in the sense of a *physical* offspring. To them, therefore, it's as if we were saying that God had illicit sexual relations with Mary, from which liaison Jesus issued forth as a bastard child, if you will. So if we are shocked that someone would say, 'Jesus is a bastard and his mother is a whore', perhaps we can better understand why Muslims are equally shocked by the central claim of Christianity, that Jesus is the Son of God.

From a Muslim perspective, God cannot have a *son* because he has no *wife*! The Qur'an says, for example, 'The originator of the heavens and earth! How can He have a child, when there is for Him no consort . . .' (6:102). 'And [we believe] that He – exalted be the glory of our Lord – hath taken neither wife nor son' (72:3). Here, then, the words 'father' and 'son' are given a *literal* interpretation. (In other passages from the Qur'an however, those words are used *figuratively*. For example, Muhammad's uncle, Abdul Uza is called in the Qur'an, 'Abu Lahab', meaning the father of a flame.)

Apparently we haven't made clear the message that we are talking about a different concept of sonship wherein Jesus is the Son of God in a spiritual sense, expressing the perfect intimacy of relationship with God as Father. Certainly the virgin birth was a physical phenomenon in the body of Mary. Yet it is not as if God, who is spirit, had sexual relations with Mary. She was miraculously impregnated by the power of the Holy Spirit and gave birth to a man in whom all the fullness of the godhead was incarnated.

Instead of Jesus becoming one of three gods (along with God and 'the Mother'), as Muslims assume we believe, we must somehow convince them that the idea is of the One God becoming Jesus. (In person, function and purpose, God the Father above; God the Son – Jesus – below.) It is God appearing on earth in the form of a human being whom we know as Jesus.

The concept of Trinity (one God in three persons, but one in substance) is as difficult for Christians to sort out as it is for Muslims to teach that nothing can be *associated* with the eternal Allah (least of all a 'son' of God), yet believe that the Qur'an itself has existed eternally (implying, therefore, *its* association with Allah). Once we leave the natural world and attempt to explain the realm of the supernatural, all of us stand on shaky ground.

To give some indication of how far Christians are from the supposed blasphemy of Jesus being the Son of God, one can see that the Qur'an twice refers to Jesus (Isa) as 'the Word':

> . . . The angels said, 'Mary, God gives thee good tidings of a Word from Him whose name is Messiah, Jesus, son of Mary . . . (3:40).

> The Messiah Jesus Christ Son of Mary was only the messenger of God and His Word that he committed unto Mary, and a Spirit from Him! (4:168).

About 600 years before the Qur'an, the Gospel gave this affirmation:

> In the beginning was the Word, and the Word was *with* God, and the Word *was* God.

> *The Word became flesh* and made his dwelling among us. We have seen his glory, the glory of the One and Only, who came from the Father, full of grace and truth.

> For the law was given through Moses; grace and truth came through Jesus Christ (John 1:1, 14, 17 – author's italics).

Far from Jesus's being the offspring of an illicit sexual relationship between God and Mary (which would be blasphemous to Christians as well), Christians believe that 'the Word' of the Qur'an – Jesus the Messiah – was from eternity God himself. To Christians, Jesus was *more* than a prophet. In fact, he was more than simply *the* prophet. Jesus was *divine*! Jesus was *God*!

Naturally, such teaching may be so revolutionary to the average Muslim that it, too, sounds like blasphemy. However, it takes us out of the category of contemptuous characterisation, where we previously stood, and into the category of doctrinal differences, where we really stand.

The point is that blasphemy may not be as much a matter of contempt as it is a matter of misunderstanding. One would be hard pressed to argue that our American friend, Mr Ruggles, didn't understand exactly what he was conveying when he made his vilifying remarks questioning Jesus's origins and Mary's virtue. Or, indeed, that the court misinterpreted what Ruggles was intending to say. Yet it gets more complicated when two different religions are involved.

Just how politely can one say that Jesus is a bastard and get away with it? The answer to that is clear. Politeness is no defence. Yet what about making a crucial statement of Christian belief which to Muslims implies that Allah is a whoremonger? What also of the Muslims' belief that Jesus himself never claimed to be the Son of God, that it was only his disciples – and, by extension, we Christians – who make that claim. Could our very claim of Jesus's deity constitute *legal* blasphemy to Muslims? Unlikely as the ultimate consequences might seem to some, would an extension of the blasphemy laws automatically place Christians at risk of prosecution?

At a minimum, basic miscommunication and inherently conflicting fundamental beliefs might well pit Muslims against Christians unnecessarily and further divide community feelings.

Hypothesis 3: Showing Contempt For Scriptures

In his *Heroes and Hero Worship*, Thomas Carlyle said, 'Nothing but a sense of duty could carry a European through the Qur'an.' With that difficulty in mind, suppose a British publisher were to print an English edition of the Qur'an. Would he be subject to a blasphemy prosecution under our proposed statute? Perhaps you are surprised by this hypothesis. After all, the *Bible* has been translated into virtually every language on the face of the earth. So what possibly could be the objection to an English translation of the *Qur'an*?

Muslims believe that the Arabic language in which the Qur'an was originally written is itself an intrinsic part of the revelation. According to Islamic teaching, if God willed it to be an *Arabic* Qur'an then 'submission' dictates that it be not translated.

You get a slight hint of how seriously Muslims adhere to the original language when you run across twentieth-century Christians who still insist that the only genuine Bible is the King James Bible – the *Authorised* Version. Authorised by *God*, some apparently believe. From their unrelenting insistence, one would think that the Biblical writers spoke and wrote Elizabethan English!

'But are there not already English translations of the Qur'an?' someone asks. The answer is both 'yes' and 'no'. Yes, you can read the Qur'an in English if you wish to do so. No, technically there are no *authorised* English translations available. My own copy of the

Second Thoughts About Blasphemy

Qur'an illustrates the confusion. It is entitled *The Meaning of the Glorious Qur'an*. Yet its subtitle reads: 'An explanatory translation by Mohammed Marmaduke Pickthall.' To understand it properly, put heavy emphasis on the word 'explanatory' and play down the word 'translation'. Pickthall, a British Muslim, takes pains to explain:

> The Koran cannot be translated. That is the belief of old-fashioned Sheykhs and the view of the present writer. The Book is here rendered almost literally and every effort has been made to choose befitting language. But the result is not the Glorious Koran, that inimitable symphony, the very sounds of which move men to tears and ecstasy. It is only an attempt to present the meaning of the Koran – and peradventure something of the charm – in English. It can never take the place of the Koran in Arabic, nor is it meant to do so.

Reverence of the Qur'an is for its *form* as well as its *substance*. That is why you will not find a copy of the Qur'an on the floor, as you might find a copy of the Bible lying on the carpet after a home Bible study. Also, our habit of marking up our Bibles with underlining, highlighting, and marginal notes would be unthinkable to a Muslim. Not least, one can only wonder what Muslims might think of a chronologically-arranged version of the Qur'an, as I have done with the Old and New Testaments in *The Narrated Bible*!

For all these reasons, then, the more serious offence of any unapproved publication of the Qur'an, no matter how well motivated, might well prove costly under an extended blasphemy law. The purpose of this hypothetical is to show that blasphemy can mean radically different things in non-Christian cultures. In our admirable haste for equal protection and fair play, we must exercise caution, lest we be surprised by the unexpected.

Hypothesis 4: Manner Versus Content – Is It Always That Simple?

Repeatedly, we see that the most disturbing difficulty with blasphemy laws is the problem of definition. More than once, we have talked about the difference between *content* and *manner*, with manner being the key to blasphemy. Yet in the *Gay News* case, cited earlier, I wonder if we might not have skipped too lightly over that distinction. Let us suppose that a liberal Biblical scholar (unquestionably heterosexual with no personal axe to grind) were to publish in a highly-respectable theological journal a serious article on homosexuality from a Christian perspective. Would he be subject to a blasphemy prosecution if he were to put forth a case that Jesus himself was a homosexual? Given a particular jury, he might well be convicted. (Does blasphemy depend on its source? Is the same statement less blasphemous in a theological journal than it would be in a homosexually-oriented newspaper?)

I hold no brief for either *Gay News* or our hypothetical Biblical scholar. The idea that Jesus was a homosexual is plainly outrageous, both Scripturally and morally. (So why does every movie about Jesus invariably depict him as effeminate?) Yet I wonder if it isn't far too easy to blur the line between content and manner, between 'manner' and 'medium'. If it is easy to do that with an issue on which many Christians happen to share the outrage of Mrs Whitehouse, it might also be easy to do that on some other issue which would put Christians on the receiving end of a blasphemy charge. I wish it were simpler.

Second Thoughts About Blasphemy

Even if *content* and *manner* were easily distinguishable, we still face the problem of defining *manner* itself. Just how harsh may a zealous evangelist be in condemning unbelief and unfaithfulness? Would the rough and tumble language commonly employed in the arena of British politics be condemned as excessively offensive in the religious arena?

Looking back to Biblical illustrations, Jesus and John the Baptist probably would not fare very well in today's society if they insisted on using modern linguistic equivalents of 'you brood of vipers', 'you hypocrites', and 'son of hell'. Worse yet would be Elijah's scorn for Baal (implying he was relieving himself in the bushes instead of answering the prayers of his prophets). Or perhaps the Apostle Paul's suggestion that those who insist on the rite of circumcision go further and castrate themselves!

Manner and content are neighbours across a thin boundary. Unfortunately, if some blasphemy is crystal clear, other 'blasphemy' may depend upon whose bell is being rung at the time!

A Troubling Dilemma

In a pluralistic society, how can we any longer refuse equal protection under the law to non-Christian faiths, some of which may be in even more need of the law's protection? Yet with so many questions surrounding the definition and application of blasphemy laws, particularly if extended to non-Christian religions, it is difficult to support any move for such an expansion. One wants to quote the adage: 'Let a sleeping dog lie.'

As if it weren't already sufficiently confusing, there is still the important issue of free speech to consider, and the even more important matter of moral responsibility. So, take a deep breath as we take the plunge.

From harmless hypotheses, we move back into the real world – a world where a single book can be the cause of riots, the severing of diplomatic relations between nations, and the deaths of people perhaps so poorly educated that they could not even have read the book.

6

At What Cost Free Speech?

Balancing Free Speech and Respect for the Sacred

> If all printers were determined not to print anything till they were sure it offended nobody, there would be very little printed.
>
> Benjamin Franklin

As I sit at my computer and type out the words you are now reading, I haven't the slightest fear that I am in danger of being prosecuted under the laws of blasphemy. First of all, that's because I have no intention to blaspheme. It's also because, despite differences in beliefs with any number of people and recognised religions, I do not regard any of them with contempt. No matter how important I think it is to stand for the truth as I believe it to be, my integrity as a writer is not threatened by any legal limitations. My own sense of values would prevent my going so far as to have to worry about running foul of the law.

With that in mind, it is exceedingly curious to me that

coalitions of authors and writers around the world have joined in protest against Islam's charges of blasphemy against Salman Rushdie. Naturally, I – along with millions of others – join them in outrage against the late Ayatollah's death threat. The death penalty for blasphemy may be understandable within an Islamic framework, but is wholly repugnant to a non-Islamic world. However, difficult as it is, put the death threat itself aside for a moment. Let us consider separately the issue of free speech as it relates to blasphemy.

I have already expressed solidarity with those who value free expression, particularly within a pluralistic society. As an author, I have a vested interest in the free communication of ideas. However, as a law professor I can also tell you what you already know, that free speech is not without its limitations. None of us, with impunity, can cry 'Fire!' in a crowded theatre; or incite others to riot; or threaten to kill the Queen. Nor can we escape adverse legal consequences if we disclose official state secrets amounting to treason. Try making obscene telephone calls to strangers or distributing pornography to school-children and you'll quickly discover that there are some forms of expression that society simply will not tolerate. And rightly so.

Free speech is not unconditional. Despite all the rhetoric to the contrary, editors and publishers acknowledge the conditional nature of free speech in the way that they *act*. For example, are we to believe that the editors of *The Times* or *The Independent* would publish an advertisement placed by the late Ayatollah Khomeini soliciting British Muslims to kill Salman Rushdie? Would *The Sun* stoop to publish it? We should fall over from shock and disbelief if they did!

Therefore, when it comes to blasphemy, I am all the more curious that authors and writers scream so loudly about free speech, as if to *demand the right* to blaspheme the sacred! When they sit down at *their* computers, or take pen in hand, do they really believe that they are immune from the common decencies of social intercourse? Does their status as authors somehow give them a right that ordinary people do not have to cast contempt on others?

One sometimes gets the idea that authors think they have their own special revelation from above permitting them to flout all the rules the rest of us have to live by. Indeed, sometimes insensitivity (whether through obscenity or blasphemy) seems to be taken as a badge of intellectual and literary prowess.

I can possibly gather some sympathy for Mr Peter Wright, whose book *Spycatcher* was banned in Britain. Given the fact that Australia – another parliamentary democracy – gave approval to his book, the value of its suppression may be questionable. I can also understand that the arbitrary lines drawn by Lord Rees-Mogg's Broadcasting Standards Council would draw the fire of those who believe the lines have been drawn too tightly in a given area of media broadcasting. (Others will believe them too loosely drawn.)

Nevertheless, I join with those who urge that the privilege of free speech depends to *some* degree on its responsible use. And *privilege* it is, there being no *unconditional* right to free speech. As one editorial put it, 'A civilised society is unwise to insist that all abuses of freedom of expression within the law, regardless of the damage done, form part of the ark of the covenant and so are sacrosanct.' It will come as shocking news to some, but no writer has an absolute right to say what he wants. Free speech is not that free.

Ignoring Danger Signals

Have we come to the point when sensationalism at others' expense is an accepted substitute for quality literary pursuit? As expressed in his letter to *The Times*, Roald Dahl would hope otherwise: 'In a civilised world we all have a moral obligation to apply a modicum of censorship to our own work in order to reinforce this principle of free speech.'

Dahl's comment raises an important question about Mr Rushdie. Does it make sense that an author, wanting to highlight perceived injustices from the British government and the forces of Islam, then to demonstrate callous indifference to the feelings of others? Does not insensitivity *generate* insensitivity? If we demand freedom of expression for ourselves, we must come to appreciate freedom of belief in others.

My curiosity runs rampant when I think of yet another detail in the whole Salman Rushdie affair. The contract which I signed with the publisher of this book contains what I suspect is a fairly standard clause in British publishing contracts:

> The AUTHOR warrants to the PUBLISHERS that the work contains nothing objectionable, libellous, obscene, improper, scandalous, indecent, blasphemous, a breach of the Official Secrets Act or in any other way unlawful.

Interesting, isn't it, that even British publishers acknowledge the limitations on freedom of expression, and give themselves a way out of a contract should those limitations be exceeded? Did Mr Rushdie's contract with Viking-Penguin Press contain a similar clause? If so, did Mr Rushdie sign his contract in good faith? Given the financial success of *The Satanic Verses*, of course, it is not likely that Viking-Penguin would exercise their option to consider his blasphemy a breach of contract. Even so, wouldn't you love to have just a quick peep at the fine print?

I quoted earlier from Chief Rabbi Jakobovits, who

finds free speech abused on each side of the Rushdie affair: 'Both Mr Rushdie and the Ayatollah have abused freedom of speech, the one by provocatively offending the genuine faith of many millions of devout believers, and the other by a public call to murder, compounded by offering a rich material reward for an ostensibly spiritual deed.'

Although he opposes the extension of blasphemy laws to non-Christian religions, the Chief Rabbi nevertheless urges voluntary restraint, saying, 'There should be widespread agreement on prohibiting the publication of anything likely to inflame, through obscene defamation, the feelings or beliefs of any section of society, or liable to provoke public disorder and violence.' As previously mentioned, it is not as if Viking-Penguin were unaware of the potential consequences of Rushdie's book. Their own Indian editor had put them on notice of trouble ahead.

Unfortunately, Viking-Penguin ignored repeated warning lights and soon found themselves plunged into disaster. Perhaps for them the warning lights came too late in the process to put on the brakes. Perhaps they received conflicting signals. My guess is that, for virtually all of us, the warning lights simply aren't operating as they once did. Through decades of brainwashing about the unlimited right of free speech – particularly for the intellectual élite – we have been desensitised to self-restraint. We forget that the right to swing our literary fists ends at the reader's nose.

A Case of One-sided Free Speech

In a brilliant and insightful piece of his own free-swinging journalism (*The Times*, March 3rd, 1989), Bernard Levin took Mr Norman Mailer and his fellow authors to task over their self-righteous Rushdie protests. At a

New York rally, Mailer had declared that the Ayatollah had 'awakened us to the great rage we feel when our liberties are threatened'. Observing wryly that '"Liberties" may be a misprint for "royalties"', Levin went on to answer Mailer's dramatic claim that 'we are beginning to feel that we are willing to suffer, even die, for our ideals'. Levin asks: 'How do you demonstrate your readiness to suffer or die for your ideals in a society which has no vacancies, in the Help Wanted columns, for martyrs?'

The point is that it is easy to become altogether too self-righteous when risk is illusory, when commercial interests cloud one's dedication to duty, when the deep-seated faith of others never enters the conversation. To Western writers, unfettered free speech is enlightened libertarianism, whereas Eastern respect for the sacred belongs to a bygone era of ignorance and superstition.

Unfortunately, author Fay Weldon spilled the beans on all this high-handed preaching from Mailer and his crowd when she appeared as one of the guest panellists on Granada Television's programme entitled 'Hypotheticals – A Satanic Scenario' (May 30th, 1989), which explored how various public officials and community leaders would deal with imaginary situations surrounding the Rushdie affair. Said Weldon, 'Burn the book today; kill the writer tomorrow.' (So far so good.) Freedom of speech to burn a book, Fay Weldon? 'No, I find that offensive . . .' (Oops!) In other words, freedom of expression runs only one way! Western intellectuals are entitled to it, but religious zealots are not!

Whatever happened to the freedom of *others* 'to suffer, even die, for their ideals', to use Mailer's language – much less to burn a book as an expression of outrage at injustice? It's interesting how the priorities fall. Western secularist authors would die (well, theoretically speaking) to preserve the right to disrespect all things sacred, but Muslims, being religious folk, are not entitled to burn a book in protest when one of the secularists is caught doing it. It's as extremely inconsistent as Yusuf Islam (formerly Cat Stevens) saying on the same programme that he personally would not kill Salman Rushdie, but, given the opportunity, he would phone someone who would!

Sometimes I think that secularist authors fancy themselves to be intellectual squatters who can camp on whatever turf they like, no matter how offensive it is to the rest of us. Like squatters who clutter the landscape – as if called to irresponsibility by some cosmic religious mandate – 'progressive' authors seem to find some twisted satisfaction in upsetting the orderly fabric of society *for its own sake*. In those cases where the fabric of society *needs* to be upset, then one may attempt that result more forthrightly, with a willingness to accept the consequences if society fails to agree that such a need exists.

Sometimes those who claim extraordinary privilege find it coming back at them in unexpected ways. Mr Rushdie himself was greeted with journalistic contempt when the *Mail On Sunday* published an article in June 1989, claiming that Rushdie had broken his silence and defied the Iranian death threat against him. What was touted as an exclusive post-death-threat interview was actually an interview conducted on Christmas Eve, 1988 – prior to Khomeini's death threat against Rushdie. Despite apologies by the paper, Rushdie not surprisingly denounced the 'lurid and sensationalised interview'. Ironically, Rushdie may have had a taste of his own insensitivity to the feelings of others. In that light, neither news journalism nor fictional literary expression is exempt from the need for responsible self-censorship.

*

The Many Faces of Blasphemy

Thanks to the encouragement of an all-too-generous reading public, I have been fortunate to have written a number of books over the years. All of my books, like those of every author I know, have gone through excruciating editing processes. (Whole chapters have been tossed out of the window with the slightest touch of the 'erase' button.) Sometimes the editing is purely mechanical – where, for example, the manuscript is overly long for the intended size of the book. Sometimes (to my editor's chagrin) I get carried away on any number of unproductive side-tracks. Sometimes – though I never mean it to happen – my enthusiasm for the case I am presenting goes just a bit overboard. Invariably in such instances, an alert editor's red pen comes to my rescue.

I say all that to preface my reaction to publisher Matthew Evans's (Faber and Faber) contribution to the 'A Satanic Scenario' discussion. Asked by moderator Geoffrey Robertson QC if it would not have been possible to edit out forty offensive pages in Rushdie's 550-page book, Evans said blithely, 'The publisher's role is not the role of censoring the author's work.' What? I very nearly choked on my tea!

Call it 'editing' if you must, publishers are constantly *censoring* the books bearing their imprint. Often it happens for reasons as ignoble as successful marketing. Not infrequently, it happens when the publisher's lawyer pulls the plug at the prospect of having to defend the publisher in a civil action for libel. When economics becomes the issue, 'uncompromising free speech' often takes a hurried back seat. Before you've had time to say 'Salman Rushdie', out comes the censor's (sorry, *editor's*) scissors!

There is yet a greater, ongoing censorship taking place every day. Among publishers, it happens in the very act of choosing which manuscripts to publish. (Would

At What Cost Free Speech? 83

Viking-Penguin be receptive to an author who wishes to present an Islamic perspective on the issues raised by Mr Rushdie?) Among booksellers, it happens in ordering the books which will be offered to the book-buying public. (Chain bookshop head Tim Waterstone found *The Satanic Verses* offensive, but a very 'important work'.)

Among newspapers, it happens in deciding which letters-to-the-editor to publish. (Andreas Whittam Smith, editor of the *Independent*, said nevertheless, 'My duty is always to publish . . . I can't self-censor myself.') Among film producers, it happens in deciding which scripts to transform into celluloid. (Producer and director Michael Winner thought it would be all right to offend religion, if necessary, but definitely not races!)

With tongue in cheek I could mention that I'm particularly encouraged by Mr Waterstone's duty to publish 'important works' on 'important issues'. That's good to know. It will be great to see more issue-oriented, evangelical Christian books on Waterstone's shelves in the near future. (I also await with breathless anticipation the movie version of *The Satanic Verses* which I assume that some producer somewhere, compelled by the irresistible moral force of free speech, feels called to bring to the wide screen.)

Naturally I am being facetious here. As an evangelical Christian author, it doesn't surprise me that predominantly secular book publishers would have minimal interest in evangelical Christian books. Nor would it make sense for a Christian book publisher to publish trashy sex novels or even Islamic literature. The point is not that every publisher or bookseller ought to be required to welcome every book that walks in the door. The point is that there is no cause for all the pretension about censorship, or about the supposed imperative of free speech that prevents us from making judgments about the content of what gets into readers' hands.

Free speech and self-censorship go hand in hand. It

must not be overlooked that free-speech advocates like John Milton argued the case of free speech for serious works of dissent or insight which would have allowed for the Twains, Joyces, and Lawrences to speak their piece. Classic free-speech debate has never been about the kind of pornography, obscenity, racism, or blasphemy which is likely to end up in court today. The idea of free speech is freedom of scholarship, not freedom of filth or desecration of the sacred.

If the line is not always easily drawn between the acceptable and the unacceptable, nevertheless it must be drawn. It is too easy for us to say that, since we don't always know for certain where to draw the line, therefore we are entitled to draw no lines whatever. As one American jurist said regarding obscenity, 'I can't define it, but I recognise it when I see it.' Indeed, I suspect that, deep down, we also recognise blasphemy when we see or hear it. When we *do* recognise it, the question is, what are we willing to do about it?

All of us – even writers, publishers, booksellers and film producers – are our brothers' keepers. We *can* make judgments, and we *must*. Put another way, we *do* make judgments, and we should make them better. As one of the members of the panel urged, those of us wielding the power of the pen need more humility, more sense of proportion, more appreciation of the real world where everyone else lives. Although he did not always follow his own rule, at one point in his book even Rushdie engaged in self-censorship: '(delicacy forbids the publication of explicit details)' (p. 273).

As an example of self-restraint and sensitivity, I offer the recent voluntary withdrawal by a prestigious Christian publisher of a book which allegedly contained a matter of offence to an individual who threatened legal action. Note carefully the explanatory press release: 'Considering it unseemly, and unbiblical, for Christians to take matters to court, we have taken the view that it is in the better interests of the Christian Church for us to withdraw the offending edition from circulation.'

Nor was the principle of free speech threatened by this corporate act of conscience. The publisher simply reprinted the book, excluding the 'offensive' material. Would it not have been possible for Viking-Penguin to make a similar gesture of goodwill with *The Satanic Verses*?

The Flip-side of Free Speech

When free speech is exalted (and may it ever be), we must nevertheless recognise that it is only one of many facets in a cluster of personal fundamental rights guaranteed to people in a free society. Another, equally-important facet in that same cluster of rights is *religious* freedom. In one sense, free speech itself encompasses freedom of religion, for both are guaranteed rights of expression. Both are extensions of the even more fundamental freedoms of thought and belief which underlie judicially-recognised guarantees. Yet, oddly enough, these two freedoms do not always run along parallel tracks.

Where the non-believer has a right of free speech, it is possible for that right to be exercised at the expense of a believer's religious freedom. In order for religious freedom to remain vibrant, the believer must be protected from the inhibiting effect of religious insult. If there can be a 'chilling effect' on free speech, there can also be a 'chilling effect' on the free exercise of religion.

In the cluster of human rights, one freedom must not be allowed to diminish yet another freedom. It is here, in the conflict of freedom of speech and freedom of religion, that blasphemy laws may provide an important buffer at the point where the two freedoms tend to come into conflict. Blasphemy laws place limitations on unbridled free speech which would threaten freedom of religion through insult or disrespect. Blasphemy laws are a reminder that one person's right of free speech is another person's right of religious freedom.

And there is this intriguing thought to consider. Deriving as they do from the same fundamental source, freedom of speech and freedom of religion tend either to stand or fall together. If the latter is diminished, so too will be the former. (A quick check of totalitarian governments will confirm that conclusion.) Seen in that light, blasphemy laws can actually be a pillar of support for free speech!

A Celebration of Blasphemy

The battle of the Rushdie affair is not between censorship and free speech. The battle is between faith and contempt for faith. Never was this made clearer than in Tony Harrison's 'The Blasphemers' Banquet', shown on July 31st, 1989, in BBC-1's 'Byline' series. Touted as a challenge to bigots everywhere (with the subtle implication that anyone having faith is a bigot), 'The Blasphemers' Banquet' was just what the title implied: a celebration of blasphemy against all religion.

This 'spirited defence of free speech' was, as Charles Spencer put it (The *Daily Telegraph*, August 1st, 1989), 'a hymn to atheism . . . a defiant raspberry blown in the face of fundamentalism, whatever the religion involved'. Although it purported to speak out against the ugliness of religious fanaticism, Spencer recognised that 'If the work had a fault, it was Harrison's refusal to see *any* good in *any* religion.' And, of course, that is the point.

One would hardly cast mainline Presbyterians as religious fanatics, yet a former Presbyterian church building used now as a Tandoori restaurant was depicted as a symbol for Harrison's belief that secular pleasures are to be preferred over vague promises of joys in heaven.

At What Cost Free Speech? 87

It was not a defence of free speech as much as a case for 'Eat, drink, and be merry, for tomorrow we die' versus 'Pie in the sky when you die by and by'. And almost that shallow, I'm afraid.

The 'gimmick' of the programme was to invite to the banquet Molière, Voltaire, Byron and Omar Khayyam – all dead and gone – and Salman Rushdie – who, due to the death threat hanging over him, could not attend. The point somehow was to associate Rushdie with the revered writers who had gone before him, all of whom had been reviled by the religious during their lifetimes. What they had in common, supposedly, was the courage to speak freely about religion and non-religion. Yet it is not surprising that the final toast to Salman Rushdie was a toast, not to free speech, but to unfettered blasphemy. Blasphemy *as* blasphemy!

I've just reread Omar Khayyam's *Rubaiyat*. It is an ode to drink and merriment in the joy of the moment as a preferred alternative to the after-life promised by religion to those who would forgo some of this world's pleasures. Perhaps Omar Khayyam's philosophy is best captured in these words:

> Ah, make the most of what
>   we yet may spend,
> Before we too into the Dust
>   descend;
> Dust into Dust, and under
>   Dust, to lie,
> Sans Wine, sans Song, sans
>   Singer, and – sans End!
>   (XXIII)

I dare say that this Epicurean philosophy is cold comfort to an author presently unable to enjoy the 'good life' because of what he has written. Other, more familiar, words from the *Rubaiyat* must now be a haunting refrain to Salman Rushdie:

> The Moving Finger writes;
> and, having writ,
> Moves on: nor all thy Piety
> nor Wit
> Shall lure it back to cancel
> half a Line,
> Nor all thy Tears wash out a
> Word of it.
>
> (LI)

Free speech, as a purist ideal, would permit Omar Khayyam's unbelief. It would also permit even religious fanatics their belief. If Khayyam is right – that this life is a dead-end street – why should his cup of wine be any more exalted than others' religious faith? Neither is less to be championed in the end. If he is *wrong*, of course, then faith may yet be vindicated.

More to the point, however, is the fact that the whole of the *Rubaiyat*, disdainful as it is of the notion of Paradise or after-life, does not begin to touch the blasphemy of *The Satanic Verses*. Where the *Rubaiyat* expresses one man's personal *belief* in the futility of religious faith, *The Satanic Verses* expresses one man's *contempt* for the personal beliefs of others in the importance of their religious faith. Omar Khayyam *rejects* faith; Salman Rushdie *mocks* faith. *Rejecting* faith is a matter of free speech; *mocking* the faith of others (and more especially the one they revere as God's messenger) is blasphemy.

In crossing the line from free speech to unrestrained blasphemy, Rushdie the secularist has grasped for the only possible reward – posterity, not eternity: his own distinction in *The Satanic Verses*: 'The writer agrees to the ruination of his life, and gains (but only if he's lucky) maybe not eternity, but posterity, at least' (p. 459). How little Rushdie will have achieved for all his contempt. And at what cost! Certainly nothing to celebrate. Hardly worth a banquet.

7

Whether to Abolish

The Role of Legislation in Safeguarding the Sacred

> Statutory law is based upon common law; common law is based upon moral law; and moral law is based upon divine law.
>
> **Anon**

In previous chapters we have struggled with what a blasphemy law ought to look like in terms of the acts and intents which might be prohibited. The underlying assumption was that blasphemy laws are a good idea – at least, in the view of many, if extended to non-Christian faiths as well. There are those, however, who urge that blasphemy laws ought to be abolished altogether. Tony Benn's Bill, for example, is only the latest of several attempts over the years to do away with blasphemy laws. The first Bill to abolish was drafted by Mr Justice Stephen in 1884. Another attempt failed in 1930, as did mounting pressures in the mid-1950s.

Civil libertarians have argued over the years that the

very existence of blasphemy laws sets up a 'chilling effect' on free speech. They contend that a person should not have to worry about being criminally prosecuted for accidentally going too far with humour, satire, or fictitious comment regarding matters of religion, but the history of the blasphemy laws over the past century – less than a dozen cases – indicates little cause for panic.

In that light, of course, one might wonder if there is a real need for such laws. At the least, it can be said that Christianity has carried on over the years without having constantly to protect itself from scurrilous attacks from its critics. Other religions – among them, Islam – have actually flourished quite well without equal protection under the laws. One might also suppose that Islam will continue to flourish despite the Rushdie slur. Indeed, perceived persecution often galvanises a body of believers in a way that fashionable acceptability never can.

Yet it is surprising how many scores of statutes are rarely prosecuted, not the least of which, for example, are the laws of treason. How many threats to the life of the Queen might we suppose have been made over past years? Relatively few, I should guess. Yet are we ready to abolish the laws prohibiting such threats? Sometimes the very presence of a law is sufficient to deter the prohibited conduct.

On the other hand, the rarity of prosecutions might also cause some to wonder aloud if we aren't setting ourselves up for selective prosecutions in sensational cases. Who wants to bask in the security of thinking that nothing is ever done about blasphemy, only to receive a surprise summons? Of course, it just might be the odd sensational case – perhaps like that of Rushdie – where the sheer breadth and seriousness of the harm done might justify such a prosecution. Perhaps we need to keep the law in reserve for that special case which truly ought to reflect the public's outcry.

Whether to Abolish

In the light of widespread religious apathy among the Christian community, others would ask: if no great hue and cry is caused by an insult made against God or the Christian faith, of what value is the continued retention of the blasphemy laws? The immediate answer is that, if the Christian community has lost its sensitivity to the sacred, there are other communities which obviously have not lost that sensitivity. Rather than abolishing the blasphemy laws, we may have cause once again to consider *extending* them. Particularly might that be true where the affected community happens to be principally a racial minority, already vulnerable to unjust attack.

Sending the Wrong Signal

It doesn't come from an unexpected quarter, but caution from at least two Christian leaders is worth considering. In an interview with Barbara Amiel regarding the role of women in the church (*The Times*, December 12th, 1988), the Bishop of London, Graham Leonard, touched on the more general issue of disestablishment of the Church of England, and on blasphemy laws in particular:

> I would say that the significance of disestablishment is totally different from the position which you would have had if the Church had never been established. This applies to any legislation. I mean, to remove the law against blasphemy is totally different from never having had a law against blasphemy. If it's removed, people immediately think it's all right.

He's right about that, isn't he? When a law is abolished we tend to assume that the reason behind the law in the first place has somehow vanished.

It would be easy to dismiss the opinions of a churchman as defending an entrenched position of blind vested interest on behalf of the Church, but Graham Leonard makes an interesting concession which lends credibility to his bottom line conclusion:

> I think most of us wish there had never been a law on blasphemy. On the whole, you see, I have a fairly low expectation of legislation. You can't make people good by legislation.

Perhaps, however, Leonard has conceded too much too quickly. The old standby that 'you can't legislate morality' has a sting in its tail. It is certainly true that if people want to do something badly enough, they will do it regardless of what laws happen to exist. We need only look at America's futile attempt to prohibit the use of alcohol, depicted in those great reruns of Elliot Ness and *The Untouchables*. However, that is not the end of the story. The truth is that legislation does affect morality in fairly widespread ways.

Consider, for example, the broad set of laws aimed at so-called 'victimless crimes'. Laws against drug use and prostitution (add gambling in most American states) are directly related to issues of morality. If there are those who flout those laws in the face of prohibitive legislation, there are countless others who don't – simply because it is illegal. Think also of laws protecting underaged females from sexual exploitation, and laws restricting abortion. Even laws which govern fair weights and measurements are designed to guard against the immorality of cheating. For that matter, virtually *all* criminal laws trace their way back to laws of morality found in the ancient Laws of Moses.

From a spiritual perspective, Dr Leonard is right that 'You can't make good people by legislation'. Unfortunately, it is not always the 'good people' we are concerned about. In fact, laws are designed principally with people in mind whose own standards of conduct are beneath those of the community. For them, laws can and do create expectations and make demands – and *deter*. Even for the most circumspect among us, laws set a tone to remind us of who we are and how we ought to act. It is here that Dr Leonard is dead right: a change in the law invariably sends a signal. In the case of blasphemy laws, as in the case of laws once prohibiting homosexual activity, it might well be a powerful signal indeed.

Leonard's colleague Dr John Habgood, Archbishop of York, concluded the letter we earlier referred to with this observation about how writers likely would interpret any mid-course change of direction:

> The simpler alternative of abolishing the offence of blasphemy altogether would be to signal, however inadvertently, that in the last resort our society holds nothing sacred, apart from the freedom of writers to write whatever they like. This is, for obvious reasons, attractive to writers, indeed is asserted by some with quasi-religious fervour. But important though it is, why should it have absolute priority over all other claims to sacredness?

Habgood has cut right to the heart of the matter. It's a question of what signal we are making. One might easily concede that a democratic society – even a *Christian* society – can thrive well enough in the absence of blasphemy laws. The United States – a bastion of free speech, for good or for evil – immediately comes to mind. One might even suggest that the absence of an established Church, which current blasphemy laws mirror, would be an asset to the vibrancy of the Christian faith. Certainly Christianity in America, admittedly with its own set of problems, is still alive and well despite (because of?) having no official state Church.

Context cannot be ignored, however. The fact is that

Britain has had blasphemy laws for centuries. Abused as they too often have been, they have long stood as a reminder of community expectations and been a significant part of the constitutional bulwarks which have protected the values of a strong civilised society. What statement would be made if blasphemy laws were abolished after all these years, particularly at a time when secular humanism is waging a tireless war of attrition against once-revered values?

It's not a matter of perpetuating tradition which no longer has relevance to a changed society. Nor is it opposing a reasonable change for no better reason than that those with a different world view happen to support it. Current blasphemy laws, even unenforced, have become symbolic of a much larger issue. With respect for a sense of the sacred on offer in an increasingly godless society, the concern here is that we do not send the wrong signal.

What signal, for example, is Tony Benn hoping to send? Does he share the same sense of the sacred as Graham Leonard and John Habgood? Is it the *laws* against blasphemy which most offend him, or the concept of *blasphemy itself*? One who appreciates the outrage of believers (of whatever faith) at expressions of contempt for things held sacred is not likely to be offended at the presence of laws prohibiting it.

There may be any number of practical reasons why many people – including Christians and Muslims – might support the abolition of blasphemy laws in this country. Yet let us not delude ourselves about the motives of many others. The 'conspiracy' so greatly feared by Muslims is not a conspiracy of the Western world against Islam, but the forces of secularism against all that is held to be sacred, be it Islamic or Christian. To the intellectual élite, atheists and secularists, the blasphemy laws are coveted territory in the ongoing battle for faith.

Towards a Greater Concern

I confess that, for me, the dilemma about blasphemy laws persists. On the one hand, I believe that Christian-oriented blasphemy laws are no longer defensible. Associated as they are with an established Church, not even those of us from other Christian fellowships can feel really good about them. Moreover they reflect a Church-state relationship which lives more in history than in the present.

On the other hand, for the many reasons I have stated, a move to extend the protection of blasphemy laws to other religions is also fraught with problems – some hypothetical and remote, some practical and immediate. The saving grace for such legislation is that prosecutors, judges and juries have yet to run wild prosecuting legal blasphemy. With all its faults, the justice system works surprisingly well. It is not likely that new blasphemy laws, however worded, would fall into some great or regular abuse. Ironically, the religious apathy which has seized this society is the best protection both believers and non-believers have against any such abuse.

Therefore, I could live with an extended blasphemy law as a continued societal expression of respect for things sacred. In fact, despite my many misgivings as to the details of definition and application, I should applaud a conscious decision to keep blasphemy laws on the books – particularly if it followed informed, free-spirited public debate. It would be refreshing to see such a lofty national expression.

On the other hand, if the decision went the other way – to abolish the blasphemy laws altogether – I can tell you that it would make only the slightest difference to the much greater problem. The real issue is not whether to have blasphemy laws and, if so, what kind. The real issue is whether we recognise blasphemy when we see it, and, if so, how we feel about it. Are we truly *outraged*?

The greater concern is not legal but spiritual. Christianity propped up only by legislation will decay and fall into ruin. Christianity lived in the face of even hostile legislation will thrive well enough – even *grow* if carefully nurtured from within.

Enough talk, then, of laws and legislated morality. What are the *spiritual* challenges regarding blasphemy?

A Sense of the Sacred

As we begin the second half of the book, our focus will move away from a discussion of the many issues surrounding specific blasphemy laws to a much broader view of blasphemy. Here we shall attempt to get some grasp of what it means to have a sense of the sacred, or indeed what it means to *violate* a sense of the sacred. Our first stop will be in the local cinema, with particular attention given to the controversial film, *The Last Temptation of Christ*. Its similarity with *The Satanic Verses*, in both substance and style, is uncanny. Its particular brand of cinematic blasphemy involves a kind of historical distortion which insults the divine by lowering deity to mere humanity: Jesus *the man* was no more a son of God than you and I. Instead of God becoming man in the person of Jesus, a man *became* divine.

Next, we take a look at the public pronouncements and books of liberal theologians, such as David Jenkins, the Bishop of Durham, where we discover a surprisingly similar variety of blasphemy. However, in this case the historical distortion is aimed at Scripture – the *written*, rather than *incarnate*, word of God. This unlikely source of blasphemy insults God by lowering his divine revelation to the level of human philosophy.

Whether to Abolish

Moving ever more closely to the least likely source of blasphemy – the Church itself – we shall examine what could be called 'theological blasphemy'. Here we shall see that the appeal to human tradition as opposed to scriptural precedent and pattern brings us to a kind of blasphemy that operates on the other end of the continuum from liberal theologians. Whereas many liberal theologians would lower divine revelation to the level of human philosophy, 'theological blasphemy' attempts to elevate Church tradition to the level of divine revelation.

In each instance the blasphemy is found in the disrespect shown for God's full and complete revelation. In each instance, appeal is made to a kind of 'latter-day' revelation, whether it be human philosophy or human tradition. What Christians reject in the claimed 'latter-day' revelations of Islam and Mormonism, for example, we all too easily find growing wild in our own back gardens.

In this regard, a case will be made for the primacy of Scripture and why we need to take Scripture more seriously. It will centre on the fact that Scripture reflects the mind of God, not the mind of man, whereas Church traditions reflect the mind of man, not necessarily the mind of God. It will mirror Jesus's words to the critical Pharisees whose own religious traditions had shown contempt for God's revealed will: 'You have let go of the commands of God and are holding on to the traditions of men . . . Thus you nullify the word of God by your tradition that you have handed down' (Mark 7:8, 13).

The next stop takes us to a somewhat different concern than blasphemy against either the person of God or his divine revelation. Here we shall struggle with the idea of *sacrilege*, not so much as a defence of sacred institutions or doctrines, but as a caution against misplaced priorities. We shall look to see whether, as Christians, we have become caught up in various forms of Christian expression which are unworthy of the Gospel of Christ.

Specifically, we shall compare costly efforts at maintaining external sacred symbols (such as deteriorating cathedrals and abbeys) with efforts at extending the Kingdom of God (through spiritual shepherding of the Church and evangelistic outreach to others). We shall scrutinise the Church's involvement in political affairs, asking ourselves whether such involvement advances the Gospel or is, in fact, unworthy of it. What we shall hope to show is that profaning the sacred through a reversal of spiritual priorities is a far more serious concern than profaning the sacred by scribbling graffiti on church walls. While we readily recognise the latter as sacrilege, we rarely stop to consider the greater affront to the sacred mission of the Church which comes from our own misplaced priorities.

In the light of the spiritual vacuum begging to be filled in this nation, it is almost impossible to ignore a supremely-threatening form of blasphemy rapidly working its way from America to Britain. The so-called 'New Age Movement', the fastest-growing belief system in Western culture, offers us a tempting smorgasbord approach to personalised religion, but more importantly a new definition of God. That definition? You and I *are* God! If you have not heard of it yet, the New Age Movement promises to be arguably the most open and respectable form of blasphemy the world has ever known.

It is easy – perhaps *too* easy – to see blasphemy in secular books and films, or even in the Church. In the final pages of this book, we want to put the spotlight on ourselves, to take a serious look at ways in which each of us, consciously or unconsciously, might be guilty of blasphemy. If in no other way, many of us may be playing fast and loose with God's name, carelessly profaning it in our day-to-day speech.

Whether to Abolish

Yet, profane speech pales in comparison to the far more serious refusal to seek the grace of God in our lives. Such a wilful refusal – in effect setting ourselves in the place of God rather than submitting to his lordship – is a form of *spiritual* blasphemy wherein we dethrone the God of heaven in our hearts. Of all the blasphemies, legal or otherwise, this is the blasphemy of greatest eternal consequence. For it was this blasphemy which Jesus condemned as unforgivable.

With such serious repercussions at stake, we close the book with a look at the tension between pluralism and intolerance as it relates to the many forms of blasphemy and sacrilege with which we are confronted. If we are duty-bound to protest against blasphemy wherever it is found, how is that to be done to the glory of God? In what ways can we 'cleanse the temple', whether in society at large or in the Church in particular? Whatever answers might become apparent, nothing is clearer than that we must begin in our own hearts. It is there, in our hearts, that the battle for faith will be won or lost. It is there, in our hearts, that we must discover and renew a sense of the sacred.

8

Blasphemy on the Screen

Is Contempt Saved by Artistic Licence?

> Shrink not from blasphemy – 'twill pass for wit.
> —Byron
> *English Bards and Scotch Reviewers*

Time magazine said it 'touched off the angriest religious debate in years'. *Newsweek* said it 'roused the fury of the religious right, setting off a tempest the likes of which has not been seen since the Roman Catholic Church attempted to suppress Roberto Rossellini's *The Miracle* back in 1948'. America's former 'Moral Majority' leader and fundamentalist, Jerry Falwell, called it 'Hollywood's last hour'. Even Israel banned it for being insensitive and offensive. Yet Martin Scorsese, the film's director, wonders why everyone got so upset when 'it's just a movie'. Was *The Last Temptation of Christ* 'just a movie'?

Jesus's life has a long history in films, starting in 1916 with D.W. Griffith's *Intolerance* and Thomas Ince's *Civilization*. The first *Ben-Hur* was filmed in 1926 without sound. Because film-makers deemed Jesus too holy to be viewed face-forward, audiences were treated to 'long shots' and brief glimpses of his arms or legs or other partial views of 'God made flesh'.

Later, in the 'fifties and early 'sixties, *The Robe* (a hugely successful adaptation of *Ben-Hur*), a remake of *King of Kings*, and *The Greatest Story Ever Told* continued to portray Jesus in the traditional reverent light. As film critic Michael Singer put it, most of these 'religious films' brought 'genuine power and hushed beauty, even poetry' to the screen.

By contrast – to the extreme – came Monty Python's *Life of Brian*, a spoof of the period in which Jesus lived. Although Jesus is seen only briefly in the background of a scene giving the Sermon on the Mount, the character of Brian takes on every bit the mocked image of our Saviour.

Life of Brian mixes the vulgarity of profane language with scenes held to be sacred from Scripture; scorns Jesus through mockery of his healings; ridicules Christ's teaching; and makes a sham of the whole idea of crucifixion. It has its own unbiblical message: Don't follow anyone; choose for yourself how you want to live your life. And, pushing blasphemy to its limits, makes light of blasphemy itself!

According to Michael Singer, *Life of Brian* is 'never boring, always blasphemous ... and unquestionably deeply offensive to fundamentalists of any faith'. Yet, compared to *Last Temptation*, it played virtually untouched by controversy. This may be because *Life of Brian* claims (with increasing futility as the film progresses) to focus on another central figure, Brian. *Last Temptation* focuses on our Lord.

Did Scorsese not appreciate the offence his movie would give to most Christians? Perhaps, of course, he relied on the fact that there had been no uproar over publication of Nikos Kazantzakis' book itself in 1955.

More likely, he sought comfort in the opening disclaimer (added only in response to the Christian community's opposition before the movie's release) that the viewer was about to see a fictitious account of Jesus, unrelated to the Gospels. However, it would have taken a schizophrenic mind to miss the intended (if distorted) parallel between the Jesus of the Gospels and the Jesus of the movie. Call the movie fictitious. Call it hypothetical. It is still about the Jesus whom Christians believe to be their Saviour.

Of course, proof of the intended connection (and of the hollowness of the disclaimer) is found in Scorsese's explanation of why he made the film: so that we could better understand the human side of Jesus (obviously the Jesus of the Gospels). Nor must Scorsese's understanding of Jesus's *humanity* be quickly glossed over. To Scorsese, a *human* Jesus is a *fallible* and *sinful* Jesus.

Distortion of the Divine

What of the movie itself? What was so offensive? We should do well to examine, then look beyond, the more sensational dream sequence which got all the bad press. While Jesus is hanging on the cross, he supposedly is tempted to have a 'normal' life instead of giving himself in death as a sacrifice for mankind's sin. His 'normal' life consists of taking a wife and having sexual relations. As the 'temptation' continues, Jesus remarries after his wife dies and then (not so 'normally') commits adultery with his second wife's sister.

Giving Scorsese the benefit of the doubt in attempting to grapple with how the Son of God could be tempted, the adultery bit is more than incidental blasphemy. Wholly unnecessary to the statement supposedly being made, it becomes *gratuitous* blasphemy – blasphemy for its own sake!

Remember, of course, that these events do not actually occur. The dream is only a 'temptation' which Satan has hurled in his path. As Jesus nears death, his Apostles approach him, questioning why he has forsaken their plan. Ultimately, Jesus asks God to put him back on the cross to be sacrificed for mankind. He has resisted *the last temptation*!

In a sense, the dream sequence itself is so far-fetched and unbiblical that it may be the *least* offensive part of the film. Its blasphemy is an unholy mixture of the divine and the profane. Yet the greater damage had already been done, beginning with a misrepresentation of the nature of Jesus's struggle on the cross. His struggle was not with temptation, but with the burden of taking the punishment for our sins and being separated from the Father at the moment of death. What should have been the ultimate human struggle, Kazantzakis and Scorsese managed to trivialise altogether. *That* is the real blasphemy. Trivialising the sacred.

This we see all through the film. The Jesus of the movie constantly questions his divine instincts. He says he hears voices which he can't understand. At times he falls on the ground writhing in pain. He says that God tells him the plan only a little at a time. Hardly the Jesus of John chapter one, the Word who, in the beginning, was *with* God and *was* God. Hardly even the boy of twelve who knows he must be about 'his Father's business'.

The Jesus of the cinema is constantly changing his purpose. First he wants to teach love. Then he teaches the killing of the Romans. Finally he chooses to die on the cross. At one point, Judas – portrayed as a hero rather than a villain – tells Jesus to make up his mind. I have to admit I was thinking the same thing by that point in the over-long, tiresome farce.

What interested Scorsese 'was that the human part of Jesus would have trouble accepting the divine'. I suggest we need to stop worrying about the human part of Jesus accepting the divine. What we need to worry about is mankind accepting both the human Jesus who 'has been tempted in every way just as we are', and the divine Jesus who 'yet was without sin' (Heb. 4:15).

The Ultimate Blasphemy

What we have seen in this brief review of *The Last Temptation* is merely symptomatic of the greater blasphemy which pervades the entire film. It is made all the more pernicious by its subtlety. It has to do with Jesus, at the age of thirty, finally coming to realise that he is divine – just as *we* can discover our own divinity and thereby find salvation. The idea is that it is not God who will save us – it is we who will save ourselves. It is no surprise, then, that the movie ends with Jesus on the cross. There is *no resurrection* of the Saviour of the world who, by overcoming death, proved himself to be more than human, more than a spiritual struggler who manages to find the divine spark within himself.

The message of the movie is not about God who became man (Jesus), but about man (all of us) becoming God. Bingo! The ultimate blasphemy! If Jesus could realise his divinity, each of us can. If he could save himself, we too can save ourselves. If God called Jesus to be Christ, in no less a way he has called us to be our own Christ. The 'dream sequence' is benign compared with this lethal teaching. This is not just some 'art form' or 'artistic interpretation'. *This is another gospel.* A heretical gospel, certainly, but also a *blasphemous* gospel of the highest order, for it reduces the Son of God to the place of man and sets man in the place of God.

Outrage and Reaction

When Salman Rushdie presented in *The Satanic Verses* a thinly disguised portrayal of Muhammad as a somewhat hesitant, conniving prophet, he received a death sentence from the Ayatollah. If the parallel had run its course, film director Martin Scorsese would have been met with a death threat from the Pope for *The Last Temptation of Christ*, a cinematic presentation about a doubting, lunatic, lustful Jesus. As it was, elements of the Christian community both in Britain and America dramatically reacted to a cinematic portrayal of Jesus which was seen to be blatantly blasphemous, as did Muslims in the later Rushdie affair.

From the point of view of those who objected so vociferously to the film, one vital question is why *ethnic* minorities ostensibly are protected from racial slurs (in fact they probably aren't), yet *religious* groups have to tolerate such derogatory and inflammatory presentations of God. It takes us back to Michael Winner's frank distinction between racism and religious offence, the latter being acceptable, if necessary. Is that because racial differences (a verifiable fact) are legitimate interests, while religion (a matter of faith) is not?

To the credit of most Christians, the relatively peaceful pickets outside theatres showing *The Last Temptation* stood in stark contrast to bloodshed in Tehran and Islamabad. Perhaps all it means is that Christians are less outraged at blasphemy. Typically, we are offended, but not *outraged*; hurt, but not *horrified*; insulted, but not *infuriated*!

On the other hand, perhaps it means that, for Christians, countering blasphemy against the sacred (for which God's own judgment will be imposed) comes a distant second to endangering the sanctity of human life created in God's image. Still further, it may demonstrate a different way of dealing with one's enemies. Rather than putting a bounty on Scorsese's head, Christian leaders offered to compensate financial losses which might be incurred if his film were withdrawn. Even so, a difference in Christian response did not lessen the offence.

Does Artistic Licence Excuse Blasphemy?

Unlike conversational or discursive forms of expression (usually *printed* forms), *art* forms have been protected by a notion of 'artistic licence'. For centuries, the portrayal of Biblical characters and events through art and literature has been permitted even when, for example, it involves nudity of a kind which, in any other context, might be seen as objectionable. The idea may have been that the mere association with the sacred elevates the profane beyond reproach. Unfortunately, artists who have no respect for the sacred reverse the process. Instead of using the sacred to elevate the profane, they use the profane to desecrate the sacred. The result is that, as with virtually every other form of *licence*, the tendency at the lowest level is towards *irresponsible liberty*.

In a special Christmas (1988) issue of the *Sunday Times Magazine*, Anthony Burgess pointed out yet another contrast between Islam and Christianity which bears on the issue of creating God in man's own image:

> [Muslims] are wise to insist on the facelessness of their prophet who, transcending biography and iconography, inspires awe. Jesus Christ no longer does that. He is to be seen on the big or small screen as all too human. *Jesus Christ Superstar* was a wretched vulgarisation. Scorsese's *The Last Temptation of Christ* offends merely because it is logical: if Christ was a man he had the instincts of a man, including the sexual one.

But any attempt to make Jesus into a hero of the media diminishes him. We may look forward to some blockbusting novel in which Christ was a transvestite, a hermaphrodite, or a woman with a deep contralto voice. He has become mere plastic, a Palestinian eccentric who said surprising things. The Son of God? Well, we're all sons and daughters of God, aren't we, whatever or whoever God is.

What good is having a God no bigger than the width of a silver screen? Who wants a God packaged for us by those who don't believe in him in the first place? If commissioned to do so, Saatchi and Saatchi might present Jesus to us with all the excitement of a high performance automobile, but can *awesome* (which might describe a super performer on the motorway) really replace a sense of divine *awe*?

The Blasphemy of Historical Distortion

The taking of unwarranted artistic liberties can manifest itself in a number of ways, not always immediately recognisable as an assault against the sacred. The recent film *Mississippi Burning* is a good example of the controversy over the use of artistic/dramatic licence. *Supposedly* the film is fiction, but by all accounts it is based on a true historical incident. The historical incident involved the murder of two blacks and one white civil rights activist in the southern States. The crime was solved when a 'supergrass', who was paid $30,000, turned over evidence to the prosecution.

In the movie, by contrast, *two white*, and *one black* civil rights activists were murdered, and the crime was solved when, as a matter of conscience (and a touch of romance with an FBI agent), a woman obligingly points the finger at her own husband, no less. Why the changes?

Also, why were the heroes of the film two white federal agents? It is no secret that the civil rights movement was led primarily by black Americans. In fact, it is widely known that the FBI's director at the time, J. Edgar Hoover, was a staunch opponent of the movement, so why are the two heroes *his* men? Because of these obvious distortions of fact, there was outrage among many people, both black and white, at the use of 'artistic licence' in a popular film to destroy history.

The charge was that the movie's producers had desecrated what, to many people, was a movement with an almost sacred purpose, simply to put money in white people's pockets. The response from the producers of *Mississippi Burning* was that they had a story that needed to be told. Moreover, yes, in order to make the film economically viable they were forced to consider the tastes and demographics of the film-going audience. Many more white people were likely to see the film if there were more white actors.

As one who grew up in Texas, Oklahoma and Alabama during the period of segregation, I can tell you that *Mississippi Burning* portrays that era in the South faithfully and realistically. Whatever changes may have been made to make the film commercially viable did not detract from the film's message about that pivotal period of racial conflict. The film *honoured* the era. And the civil rights movement. And blacks.

For me, there is an immediate comparison to be made. As one who knows the backroads of the Gospels as intimately as I do the tensions of the 1960s in the south, I can tell you that *The Last Temptation* did *not* honour the life of Jesus. Or his message. Or Christians.

I mention the film *Mississippi Burning* in some detail in order to place the outrage against *Jesus Christ Superstar* and *Life of Brian* in a wider context. There may be legitimate reasons to object strenuously to a film other than the more ordinary reasons related to censorship of pornography or suppression of blasphemy in some technical sense.

The harsh critics of *Mississippi Burning* realise that movies have a powerful effect on film-goers' images of people and history, and recognise that it is dangerous to have outsiders rewriting a particular group's history. If the rewriting in *Mississippi Burning* was benign (as I believe it was), rewriting history can be absolutely sinister in religious movies, where the word 'sacred' has its ultimate meaning.

Distorting One's Eternal Destiny

If accepted at face value, *Jesus Christ Superstar*, *Life of Brian*, and *Last Temptation* have all those same potentials. They are distortions of both Jesus and history that, if not viewed critically, have serious harmful consequences. I realise that some Christians claim that the movie was uplifting. They agreed with Scorsese's justification for the film:

> You make Jesus accessible, and you make people understand that he knew what we go through. Then you can accept the philosophy and the ideas of Jesus.

Without questioning how far this process has led Scorsese himself into faith, who can doubt that Christianity has too often so overemphasised the spiritual identity of Jesus that we have rendered his role as God in the *flesh* and the one who 'was *tempted* yet without sin' almost meaningless? I, too, have wondered what went through Jesus's mind when a beautiful woman of Palestine walked by. Nevertheless, what call is there to go to the opposite extreme of debasing his divinity in order to make that important statement?

In contrast to believers who often need to be reminded of Jesus's humanity, I also know that many *un*believers with whom I have spoken about it thought *Last Temptation* was a great film, principally for the reason that it confirmed their own image of Jesus. They *wanted* a weak, human Jesus, and that is exactly what Scorsese gave them. Instead of focusing on the historical Jesus (God incarnate) so that we can be more closely conformed to his image, we create on the screen a celluloid God made in our own image.

Of course the danger in this kind of patronising interpretation of Jesus is not that just any historical figure is being misrepresented, but that it is the *Son of God*! Someone might say, 'But that is the whole point. *You* believe that he was the Son of God, but not everyone else does, and that is the issue Scorsese was addressing – a legitimate issue at that!' It is certainly a legitimate issue, but on what basis shall we decide the answer to the issue? Will it be on the basis of a film which, under the pretence of artistic licence, presents Jesus radically different from the way in which he is represented in Scripture? After all, it is not as if two people sit down and read the same Gospel accounts of the life of Jesus and come up with different conclusions about the nature of the man.

What we are risking is that the issue will be decided upon the basis of a sceptic's biased cinematic presentation, and that people will make crucial choices about Jesus on the basis of misinformation (a charge to which sometimes we Christians must also plead guilty).

Particularly is that true in a day when Biblical illiteracy runs rampant, when the typical movie-goer doesn't have a sufficient understanding of Scripture with which to make any valid comparisons. Hence also the reason why so many people were unconcerned about the possibility of blasphemy. Unaware of the *Biblical* Jesus, they didn't have a clue just how greatly distorted the *cinematic* Jesus really was.

Unlike many other decisions we might make about historical events, this decision can have eternal consequences. If Scorsese is *right* about an ambivalent, doubting Jesus, then at worst we Christians have invested our faith in a powerless fellow human being. On the other hand, if Scorsese is *wrong*, then others may be led to miss out on a relationship with the Eternal Being who created us and who came to earth in the person of Jesus to lead us into that sublime relationship.

Of course, even that bit of godly fluff – politely omitting as it does Jesus's own many references to hell for those who reject his teaching – is a distortion of the full message. If Jesus is telling us the truth, a wrong decision about him could mean eternal destruction of one's soul in hell. Not fashionable prose these days, I admit, but something to consider during a quiet moment of serious reverie.

Jesus was accused of blasphemy for portraying himself as God, but is innocent as charged since he *was* God. The reinvention of Jesus as a snivelling, unlikely candidate tapped by God for a divine 'Mission Impossible' ('. . . should you wish to accept it . . .') is a perversion which, although perhaps acceptable by today's artistic conventions, leaves me with the strong belief that we all ought to tear our clothes in dismay. What's more, if such aberrations are going to be tolerated and presented as mass entertainment, Christians must gain equal access to the media to remind an increasingly non-Christian society in no uncertain terms that such portrayals do not in any way present 'actual characters or events present or past'.

*

Distortions From Unlikely Sources

Let me allude momentarily to a more practical matter regarding how Christians ought to react when confronted with blasphemy. There can be no doubt that the orchestrated protests against *Last Temptation* fanned the flames of curiosity for thousands of movie-goers who otherwise would not have had the slightest interest in the film. There is a striking parallel here with the Rushdie death threat, which gave the book considerable publicity. Yet for us Christians, there is a far more serious question: Who represented Christ in the least favourable light – Scorsese, who distorted the *history* and *message* of Jesus, or the sometimes-violent and rude minority of Christian protesters who in the onlooking eyes of a secular world distorted the *meaning* of Jesus?

If perhaps a secular media might be excused for presenting the distasteful because that is what *sells*, what excuse do we Christians have for leaving the non-believing world with a bad taste about Christ's followers and, by implication, Christ himself? It doesn't matter that the non-believing world is caught up in its own hypocrisy, shouting the need for unfettered free expression while denouncing Christian protesters who are attempting to exercise that same freedom. What matters is that we give them no cause for their own hypocrisy or for dismissing Christ as the god of fanatic hooligans. There is more than one way to perpetuate a false portrayal of Jesus.

Blasphemy as an Opportunity

If distorted 'religious' movies approach or cross the line into blasphemy, there is reason for grave concern. The greatest surprise of all, however, is that there is also reason for Christian rejoicing. Such outrageous depictions of Jesus are a constant reminder that mankind simply cannot leave Jesus alone. He is a person to be reckoned with, and everyone knows it.

His very abuse is testimony to the ongoing challenge of his life and message to those who foolishly wish to assume his lordship for themselves. Unwilling to submit to him, the only remaining choice is to *crucify him afresh*. Praise God for a Saviour who makes people think! Praise God for rising up triumphantly from the grave of disdain in which they would hope to bury him. And praise God for Christ's message of salvation which is so unassailable that rebellion against it must come in the form of petty attempts at besmirching the unbesmirchable Son of God.

It remains for us as Christians to take up the challenge, to beat the sceptics at their own game, to present an even stronger case for truth and faith and personal submission. The world will always put God to the test. Blasphemy was not the invention of secular film producers and directors in the twentieth century, nor, unless the Lord hastens his coming, will it cease in the twenty-first. Blasphemy comes from hearts of disbelief. Sometimes even our own hearts.

It is there that we must put up the first line of defence. Have *we*, Scorsese-like, reduced the sinless Jesus to a carbon copy of our own humanity in order to make our own doubts and sins look better by comparison? Do *we*, in the spirit of Monty Python, take our faith in Jesus so lightly that others laugh and scorn our profession of Christianity? Which Jesus are we portraying on the stages and screens of our local communities, schools, and workplaces?

If there is to be Christian censorship, let the editing be done in the darkened recesses of our own hearts and minds. It is there we can make a difference. It is in us who believe that a faithless world can be led to honour the King, and to crown him with the respect he is due.

9

Blasphemy Among Bishops

The Threat of Unanswered Heresy

> In the hands of unbelief, half-truths are made to do the work of whole falsehoods.
>
> Enoch Fitch Burr

'Easter would not be Easter without a controversy over the theological views of the Bishop of Durham.' So begins one of the many editorials which lashed out at Dr David Jenkins following his 1989 Easter weekend pronouncement that Jesus's resurrection was not a physical resurrection but a 'spiritual experience', in the mind of the beholder both then and now. A flood of news stories and parliamentary debate came on the heels of the Bishop's dramatically-timed interview on *Inner Space*, a Tyne-Tees religious programme.

Few commentators were able to resist a comparison between David Jenkins and Salman Rushdie. Each had cast aspersions against issues fundamental to a major religion. Although using separate media, each had done it in flamboyant style. What Jenkins had going for him that Rushdie did not have was a cloak of respectability in the religious arena. He also chose a better target – a Church more intent on toleration than orthodoxy – and a blasphemer-friendly law, which winks at heresy.

Enthroned amid a cloud of controversy in 1985 for his rejection of Jesus's virgin birth and ascension, Dr Jenkins revived the furore of his critics in his latest assault against accepted Christian dogma. 'Knowing Christ is alive is an inner feeling which does not require the physical proof of a corpse coming back to life,' he told the interviewer. (Jenkins does not rule out the possibility that Jesus's body was stolen from the tomb.) 'I don't think it means a physical resurrection. It means a spiritual resurrection, a transforming resurrection. The experiencing, which enabled people to know that Jesus was alive beyond death, must be more than the revival of a corpse.'

At least two of the charges levelled against the Bishop's comments were couched in traditional blasphemy language. Some of his fellow bishops felt that Dr Jenkins's statement would *confuse* many in the Church of England. In previous centuries, to *confuse* doctrine was to blaspheme the Church and its teaching. As we know, however, the emphasis has now been switched from content to manner of presentation.

Even under this modern view of blasphemy, Jenkins has drawn fire from Peter Dawes, the Bishop of Derby, who offered that, 'although it is not the first time he has said such things, it is the polarising, *belligerent* way he has made them that I regret.' Perhaps we see yet another example of how difficult it is to define blasphemy. Surely, *belligerence* is in the eye and ear of the beholder.

*

Denying the Obvious

The Bishop is right, of course, in saying that 'To know [Christ] is alive in eternity must be more than the encountering of a ghost.' Fixing on a historical event – even the ultimate event of all history – without appreciating the spiritual implications of that event in each of our lives would be a meaningless creedal confession. Yet Jenkins's disdain for the obvious teaching of Scripture is seen in his choice of the word *ghost*. If the Biblical record is to be believed, it was not simply a *ghost* which the disciples saw.

The same Scriptures which tell us of Jesus's *crucifixion* (which the Bishop *does* feel secure in believing) also tell us that the resurrected Jesus was not just a wispy spirit playing with the minds of those who would later give up their lives for having testified to his bodily resurrection. It would be Jesus's own words that they would repeat as confirmation:

> They were startled and frightened, thinking they saw a ghost. He said to them, 'Why are you troubled, and why do doubts rise in your minds? Look at my hands and my feet. It is I myself! Touch me and see; a ghost does not have flesh and bones, as you see I have.'
>
> When he had said this, he showed his hands and feet. And while they still did not believe it because of joy and amazement, he asked them, 'Do you have anything here to eat?' They gave him a piece of broiled fish, and he took it and ate it in their presence (Luke 24:37–43).

With what foresight God has provided us – in unmistakable technicolour – a response to each assault of the sceptic!

*

Behind the Smokescreen

Jesus's *physical* resurrection is so plain that only a liberal theologian could get it as wrong as the Bishop of Durham. For liberal theologians, the problem is not with Jesus's resurrection, or virgin birth, or literal ascension. Their problem is a lack of faith in the reliability of Scripture.

Indeed, such a theologian in the person of Stanley Booth-Clibborn, the Bishop of Manchester, rushed to Jenkins's defence, highlighting for us the real point of departure for all liberal theologians: 'I think we have to see those wonderful mysterious stories of the resurrection in the light of modern knowledge and the fact that it was the faith of the disciples that produced these stories and not the other way around.'

We really can't trust what the New Testament writers tell us, they would have us believe. In fact, if we accept what they tell us, we can know as much or more today about Jesus from our own insight and experiences than was known by those first-century people who claim to have seen the nailprints in Jesus's hands!

It's an honest enough opinion, if perhaps obfuscated by a hidden agenda. Certainly these are not the first or the only clerics and scholars to find themselves denying the obvious on the pretence of more enlightened, up-to-date thinking. However, the case being put for alternative explanations of the miraculous events in the life of Jesus are, of necessity, more contrived than the questioned events themselves if taken at face value.

Moreover, the honesty of the Bishop of Durham's position is only half-truth. The other half is disclosed in his book, *God, Miracle, and the Church of England*. Take this one-two combination, for example:

> We must be clear that the Bible is a human book,

118 Blasphemy and the Battle for Faith

> witnessing to God by the Spirit of God through human means and human errors, as well as human insights (p. 15).

> The claims of the church have to be subjected to all the valid insights of a Marx or a Freud or a Durkheim (p. 15).

For Jenkins, Marx is well nigh on a par with Matthew, Mark, Luke and John! *That* is the source of the Bishop's confusion about Jesus's resurrection. Therein also lies his heresy – indeed blasphemy. We are no longer talking about a legitimate difference of opinion about what the Scriptures may tell us on a given matter of doctrine. We are talking about reducing divine revelation to the level of human philosophy. Put more graphically, it is profanity of the sacred. Moreover, given Jenkins's position of spiritual leadership, it is blasphemy *upon* blasphemy. For in abandoning the uniqueness of God's revealed Scriptures, the Bishop desecrates even the sacredness of his position.

Shifting Blame to Others

Less honest, in light of the above, is Jenkins's charge in one of his diocesan newsletters that most people in the Church manipulate the Bible, selecting texts which support their own beliefs rather than searching for the truth:

> We allege that we are concerned for the Biblical truth about this or that, but we select a text or two, usually in translation, which can mislead.
> We pay no attention either to what is elsewhere in the Bible nor to what we are doing by selecting the texts, putting this interpretation on them and insisting on this application.

Blasphemy Among Bishops

The truth of the matter is no concern of ours – our concern seems to be to claim rightness, insist on our interpretation and defend ourselves from our fears.

How can the Bishop of Durham deride others for selective 'proof-texting' when he himself doesn't even find the Scriptures historically reliable? If it weren't such a sad commentary on the shallowness of liberal theology, his all-too-apparent hypocritical censure of others would be laughable. And, oh, the affront of it all. How can anyone take more of a smorgasbord approach to the Scriptures than to dish out on to one's plate of faith a belief in the physical crucifixion of Jesus, yet contemptuously pass over the bodily resurrection (presented by the same Biblical sources) as indigestible fare!

A close look at David Jenkins's book reveals yet another irony of his high-handed charge of 'proof-texting' (of which all of us are more guilty than we should like to admit). While his book contains endless philosophising, there is precious little reference whatsoever to Scripture. Maybe the Bishop has worked out how to resolve the problem after all. In order to avoid the pitfalls of selective 'proof-texting', he simply doesn't bother quoting Scripture!

Turning Mystery Into Disbelief

Yet why should he? The truth for David Jenkins is too big for us, too *mysterious* and demanding. Church people, he says, should stop defending truths 'which are bound to be limited and partial, if they are truths at all'. Of course, if truth is that elusive, we are wasting our time appealing to the reading of Scripture, even if we cite *all* the relevant passages. The irony of Jenkins's own search for truth is that he never cites the very passages which would resolve for him many of the great 'mysteries of God'.

If he did, the mysteries would no longer be ponderous, and he would be bound to accept them as true.

In the spirit of the Bishop's call for more Scripture, let me share just these two from the Apostle Paul:

> I have become its servant by the commission God gave me to present to you the word of God in its fullness – the mystery that has been kept hidden for ages and generations, but is now disclosed to the saints. To them God has chosen to make known among the Gentiles the glorious riches of this mystery, which is Christ in you, the hope of glory (Col. 1:25–7).

> Now to him who is able to establish you by my gospel and the proclamation of Jesus Christ, according to the revelation of the mystery hidden for long ages past, but now revealed and made known through the prophetic writings by the command of the eternal God, so that all nations might believe and obey him – to the only wise God be glory for ever through Jesus Christ! Amen (Rom. 16:25–7).

Certainly God is a mystery to mere mortals. Yet the Apostle Paul assures us that what we need to know about the mystery of God has now been revealed through the Gospel of Christ. And what is central to that Gospel? The bodily resurrection of Jesus –

> For what I received I passed on to you as of first importance: that Christ died for our sins according to the Scriptures, that he was buried, that he was raised on the third day according to the Scriptures, and that he appeared to Peter, and then to the Twelve. After that, he appeared to more than five hundred of the brothers at the same time, most of whom are still living, though some have fallen asleep (1 Cor. 15:3–6).

Blasphemy Among Bishops 121

For Paul, there was no question but that Jesus's resurrection was more than simply a spiritual interaction between a heaven-absorbed Christ and the minds of Jesus's followers. Why else would he note the *simultaneous* appearance of Christ to over 500 people – people who were still available for cross-examination? To Paul's law-trained mind, the testimony of eye-witnesses to a literal bodily resurrection could have won the case in any court!

Undermining the Reliability of Scripture

Like an accused child lashing back in kind with a similar charge against his own accuser, we find David Jenkins labelling as blasphemous any firm assurance in the New Testament's reliability. From his book we read:

> If, in fact, we pretend, in the face of, for instance, careful comparison of the text of the Gospel of Mark with the text of the Gospels of Luke and Matthew that it is still possible to hold that every word of the Bible is directly dictated by God, then we are cheating and so in effect blaspheming against the God who is truth. For such a comparison shows that Luke and Matthew are prepared to exercise free rewriting on Mark (p. 15).

According to Jenkins, there is no blasphemy in challenging the bodily resurrection of Jesus, because the *real* blasphemy is in believing in the reliability of the Scriptures in the first place!

> It is apparently taken for granted that writers of the New Testament must have supposed that they were giving what we call accurate and historical reports when they preached, recollected and wrote down

the stories about Jesus. This is quite clearly a simple mistake (p. 26).

Is the Bishop telling us that the Gospel writers misrepresented the true facts? That they lied to us?

> To apply modern critical principles to Biblical stories and to find differing layers of historicity, myth, legend, and sheer embroidery is in no way to call in question either the total good faith and credibility of the writers or the validity and authenticity of their witness (p. 27).

Okay, so the Gospel writers weren't really liars. They just fudged on the facts in order to embellish their faith. Assuming that were even remotely true, how in their own day could they have got away with fudging on so crucial a fact as Jesus's resurrection? If the idea is that Jesus's own disciples stole Jesus's body from the tomb (a possibility which Jenkins accepts), how did they manage to retrieve it from the Roman guards put there to prevent that from occurring? Why wouldn't the Roman authorities have arrested the disciples for the theft?

On the other hand, if the Jewish leaders or Roman authorities had stolen Jesus's body, why would they not have produced it in order to quash the resurrection claims being made by Jesus's disciples? Liberalism is not even good logic!

Nor is liberalism in tune with the world in which the rest of us live. Jenkins's attacks on the scribal transmission of Biblical documents would lead us to believe that translation is a faulty process in itself. Perhaps, but if something is lost in the translation, it won't be the central message that falls by the wayside. There are simply too many historical safeguards for that to have happened.

Blasphemy Among Bishops

By the time you read these words, an editor at Hodder and Stoughton will have transformed my Americanisms into proper British spelling, idiom, and syntax. Yet I have no fear but that you will get the message as I intend it to be. Nor, sadly, do I fear that translators and scribes have done as much damage to the original message of the Bible as Jenkins himself. At least they regarded it as the unalterable Word of God.

Playing Into Muslim Hands

Once opened, the box of current-events blasphemies contains irony upon irony. How ironic it is, for example, that the Bishop of Durham provides theological ammunition for Islam's fundamentalist revolution and the spiritual battle against Christian belief. (Influential Muslim advocate, Ahmed Deedat, has placed Jenkins's photo on a Muslim tract, claiming Jenkins holds an Islamic view of Jesus.)

Despite apparent language to the contrary in the Qur'an itself, it is claimed by many Muslims that the original writings of the Bible have been changed or corrupted. Typical of these claims is the following passage from *Islam: Beliefs and Teachings* (1984) by Ghulam Sarwar. Note how comfortably the opening words might sit on the Bishop of Durham's own stationery:

> The Bible, as it is available today, has many incorrect things in it. Its authenticity and divinity are doubtful. It contains misleading and false stories about the Prophets. The message of Allah sent through them was either lost or distorted through neglect and folly of their followers.

> As against this, the Qur'an contains Allah's guidance for mankind in its original language, unchanged and undistorted. It restates in clear and unambiguous language the message of Allah which the followers of earlier prophets have lost. The message of the Qur'an is valid for all times and conditions (p. 30).

Not surprising, Muslims happily join with David Jenkins in denying the bodily resurrection of Jesus (Prophet Isa). Let's face it, where would Muhammad stand in the face of *that* ultimate miracle of God! Far from achieving the enhanced faith among believers which Jenkins claims to desire, he has only managed to confirm the disbelief of many others, both within the Christian community and without.

The Hidden Agenda

As with the Rushdie affair, in the Jenkins affair the deeper issues are lost in the dramatic headlines. The Bishop's quarrel is not with Jesus's resurrection, as if he were struggling – like all of us must – to comprehend fully the nature of a bodily resurrection. (How, for example, could Jesus appear in a room when the doors were locked? Why was he not immediately recognised on the road to Emmaus?) The Bishop's quarrel is with being bound 'by every word that comes from the mouth of God' (Matt. 4:4).

The problem with Jenkins is that he cannot force himself to accept the miracles of Jesus at face value and then move on to show the greater purpose for which they have occurred. He is so intent on destroying the authority of the Scriptures that he is compelled to weaken the text in any way that he can, whether by casting doubt on the Gospel stories themselves or on transmission of the text. In doing so, he empties the Gospel of its power. He flirts with human reason being of equal value as divine revelation, and borders on denying the revelation of God's mind to man. In doing that, he nudges ever so closely to the brink of blasphemy.

If ever there were any doubt about the Bishop's disdain for revelation, the case is closed when he glibly emasculates the revealed *Father* God of the Bible 'of whom', says Jenkins, 'it can be appropriately, authentically, and practically said that he (or she or it? or all three?) transacts . . . ' (p. 60). While hypocritically chiding others who would distort the *original* language of the text, Jenkins, through his own retranslation of original text, is willing to trade off respect for Scripture for whatever is trendy and fashionable in theological circles, even if that means profaning the Holy One.

What To Do About Blasphemous Heresy?

Such utter contempt for God's Scriptures is nothing less than scholastic blasphemy. It is no less so because of the fact that it is said by someone wearing a clerical collar, or speaking pious religionese, or appearing to be fashionable, nor because it is technically outside the coverage of blasphemy statutes. In fact, for all of those reasons, it is the greater blasphemy.

Surely, we should be far less concerned that a godless gay newspaper impugn the character of Jesus in order to justify the spiritual rebellion of homosexuals, or that some Saturday-night drunk might yell out that 'Jesus is a bastard and his mother is a whore'. One needs only to consider the source. By contrast, the Bishop's 'scholarly' contempt for the sacred makes theirs tame by comparison. His has all the subtlety and destructive potential of the Serpent in the Garden. All things considered, surreptitiously changing God's words is what both are about.

So what are we to do with the Bishop of Durham? Charge him with criminal blasphemy? Not a chance. Remember, heresy no longer qualifies for blasphemy. How about a gag order from Dr Runcie? I can tell you that would not sit well with David Jenkins. In fact, in his eyes that would amount to blasphemy!

> People have told me that questions which I can ask as a professor I cannot ask as a bishop, or at least I should not ask them openly. Such a suggestion appals me, and in my view comes strikingly close to blasphemy. How dare people suggest that what has to be asked about God cannot be asked in public by an authority of the church? (p. 12).

Interesting, isn't it, his use of the word *blasphemy*. Of course, the Bishop is given to a rather broad definition of the term. In the House of Lords, he has repeatedly declared the privatisation of buses to be blasphemy!

Interesting, too, his inability to see how his role as a leader in the Church calls him to a higher responsibility. Has he overlooked the Biblical qualifications for a bishop (dramatically changed as that leadership position is today)? Paul instructed Titus that a spiritual leader 'must hold firmly to the trustworthy message as it has been taught, so that he can encourage others by sound doctrine and refute those who oppose it' (Titus 1:9).

The *Daily Telegraph* (March 27th, 1989) makes an important comparison between the Bishop of Durham and Salman Rushdie:

> An important distinction must be drawn. Mr Rushdie is a layman of no standing within the Islamic faith – from which, in any case, he claims

to have lapsed. By contrast, a Bishop of the Church of England is a spiritual leader, whose pronouncements on matters of faith are supposed to deepen the belief of his flock and make the mysteries of Christianity more comprehensible. Dr Jenkins has consistently failed the test.

He would be well advised to observe Mr Attlee's injunction to Professor Laski: a period of silence on his part would be appreciated.

If criticism comes from expected quarters, it also comes from the least likely sources. Consider, for example, this editorial in *The Economist* which, despite its date of publication (April 1st, 1989), was deadly serious:

> What is odd is that this is not just any David Jenkins. It is a bishop of the Church of England: the Right Reverend David Jenkins, Bishop of Durham. Let Mr Jenkins think and say what he likes – but not as a bishop.
>
> His doubts attack the very heart of Christianity. Do his lips move, one may ask, as he recites the creed – and if so, why? A man may doubt what he chooses. Even a Christian theologian may express his doubts *urbi et orbi*, provided he speaks for himself; and the churches would be the poorer if they tried to prevent him as they used to in the past. But Mr Jenkins speaks as a bishop of his church. Why does the church let him?
>
> If the shepherds are like this, is it strange that the flock ambles around in circles, purposeless about where to go?

It is unlikely that the Church has the collective will to take the suggestion of Geoffrey Dickens, MP for Saddleworth and Littleborough: 'The Archbishops of Canterbury and York should call him in and discuss very, very seriously with him his future in the Church of England. It would certainly be beneficial if ways could be found to remove him from office.'

It is not even likely that Dr Runcie will respond to the plea of Neil Hamilton, MP for Tatton: 'When will the Archbishop of Canterbury give a lead and speak out against this man?'

I would not suggest that Jenkins be subject to either gag orders or censorship. As an individual, he has every right to air his opinions. Instead, I would hope that the Church could muster sufficient outrage to remove the Bishop from so influential a position. (Are there too many bishops who sympathise with him to make that move possible?) Short of that, I would wish for an outpouring of verbal and written responses from responsible Church leaders.

Whether *kicked* out of the Church or not, the Bishop must be *drowned* out by his colleagues. Jenkins ought to be silenced – not with a bullet as promised to Salman Rushdie – but with the Truth. The Church will not self-destruct because of one vocal radical in the ranks. It will indeed fail if the silent majority remains silent.

There is yet another way of looking at the Jenkins affair. What a grand opportunity the Bishop presents to us. For all the fuzzy-minded liberals who go about incognito, here is a man whose widely-publicised blasphemies stir the public's interest. Now is the time for *engagement*. Now is the time for serious dialogue about the issues he has raised, no matter how offensively in the eyes of some. Let's meet all the David Jenkinses of the Church head-on. If not *outside* the Church (where perhaps they might even be more comfortable), then let's blow the dust off our Bibles and let the Word of God challenge them from the pulpit.

Paul told Titus that 'there are many rebellious people, mere talkers and deceivers' who 'must be silenced, because they are ruining whole households by teaching things they ought not to teach . . . Therefore rebuke them sharply, so that they will be sound in the faith' (Titus 1:10–11,13).

Blasphemy unanswered is blasphemy condoned. Does the church have the will to fight against blasphemy in the battle for faith?

10

'Theological Blasphemy'

Profaning the Sacred Through Human Tradition

> The Bible has often been treated as if it were a wax nose which may be twisted at the whim of the interpreter.
> Clarence Tucker Craig
> *The Beginnings of Christianity*

If you like what I have said about the Bishop of Durham, don't get too comfortable. For my money, David Jenkins is also asking some very important questions, mixing his own special brand of blasphemy with at least a few statements which need to be heard. For example, he reminds us that 'we worship God, not the Church in any shape or form'. As a visitor, I must admit that I hear a lot more about what 'the Church' thinks on *this* matter or *that* than I do about what God has to say about it. This stems, I suspect, from the fact that 'the Church' as an institution in Britain has such a brooding omnipresence that one can hardly escape it.

Closely tied to that thought is Jenkins's statement that

'there is an awful lot of religion about, but very little spirituality'. In the notably irreligious nation that Britain has become, I continue to be intrigued that, compared with America (apart from its often-questionable brand of televangelism), Britain does indeed maintain a high religious profile. From the religious ceremonies at Westminster Abbey opening the legal year, to devotional sermonettes in major newspapers, to *Songs of Praise* and *Praise Be!* on TV, religion is still very much a part of British culture. Yet it is a cut-flower Christian culture, steadily wilting from having its roots severed by secularism.

At this point, efforts to reconnect religion and spirituality seem almost futile. Note, for example, calls by the former Education Secretary and others for more of a presence of religious training in the schools. What seems such a laudable goal is undercut by the question of who would be teaching such courses. The painful answer is that, in very many cases, it would be people who are only nominal Christians themselves and have no desire to instil in Britain's young people spiritual values which they may not even share. Under current proposals, Britain's children might learn more about the *history* of Jesus's ministry, yet emerge from the classroom with a David-Jenkins-type *humanistic view* of Jesus!

It reminds me of a similar situation in the States, where Louisiana attempted to force the teaching of Creation along with Evolution. Such a noble idea overlooked the fact that Creation would end up being taught by science teachers, most of whom are staunch Evolutionists! Neither a government-imposed religion, nor ritualistic traditional Christianity in the Church is ever going to instil into Britain's people a dynamic sense of the need for personal spirituality.

*

Scripture or Tradition?

That brings us to yet another area of criticism where Jenkins has hit the nail on the head:

> It is not at all evident that Church history, as a series of selective raids on the past, is a decisive guide for decisions of faith in the present and organizing for worship in the future (p. 54).

Of course, Church tradition is just one more obstacle standing in the way of what the Bishop thinks contemporary wisdom allows. So, once again, his intentions are suspect. Nevertheless, he is right about Church tradition. It should not be viewed as a basis for doctrine or Church organisation. While the New Testament provides us with a pattern because it is divinely inspired, the history of how the Church (either universally or denominationally) has interpreted and applied that pattern is far from conclusive as to issues of faith. The truth is that much of our tradition actually leads us *away from* the divine pattern.

While past tradition is to be valued as reflective of how others before us have conscientiously sought to understand the Scriptures, for that very reason tradition must always be tested by Scripture. Taking the opposite approach that interpretation of Scripture must be measured by tradition risks the primacy of human understanding over divine Truth. If Church history can put us in touch with the *best* of collective human insight, it can also make us victims of the *worst* of conventional wisdom about God and his will for man.

The context of the Bishop's remarks about Church history is the tough issue of the role of women. I know the issue is tough, because I have just completed several gruelling months researching and writing a book which addresses that issue. *Men of Strength For Women of God,* an overview of all the Biblical passages relating to this controversial subject, is 299 pages long. I mention this otherwise meaningless detail as a measure of my surprise at how little Scripture I have seen being used by Church leaders in Britain as they have debated the issue publicly. If I had limited my book to discussing the *scriptural* justification offered by Church of England authorities – on either side – I could have finished the book in under two pages!

The Bishop of Durham would not be pleased with my conclusions, reflecting as they do the consistent Biblical theme of male spiritual leadership. Yet I stand amazed at how little use has been made of available Biblical teaching on the part of the Bishop's opponents on this issue. If you pick up David Pawson's excellent book on the subject, *Leadership Is Male* (Highland Books, 1988), you get what you might expect from an evangelical Christian – a close look at what the Scriptures teach.

Whether or not you agree with Pawson's conclusions, as I do, is not the issue. The point is that he is addressing the Scriptures as if they really matter. For those in the hierarchy of the Church of England who oppose the ordination of women, the rationale is completely different. As you may have guessed, the rationale is mostly a matter of *tradition*. It is Church history as it has been handed down over the centuries. It's right principally because we have always done it this way. It's the Tevya theory (from *Fiddler on the Roof*) – Tradition! Tradition!

The assumed scriptural basis for that tradition is itself suspect. The idea is that, because Jesus chose *men* as his apostles, and because they in turn laid hands upon other *men* to empower them as priests, therefore the priesthood is an exclusively *male* club, as it were. However, hardly noticeable is a significant jump in logic from one conclusion to the next. The first wrong path down which tradition has led us is the clergy-laity distinction itself, overlaid as it is on the Biblical teaching of the priesthood of all believers. Listen again to what Peter tells us – *all* of us, whether Christian men or Christian women:

> As you come to him, the living Stone – rejected by men but chosen by God and precious to him – you also, like living stones, are being built into a spiritual house to be a holy priesthood, offering spiritual sacrifices acceptable to God through Jesus Christ.
>
> But you are a chosen people, a royal priesthood, a holy nation, a people belonging to God, that you may declare the praises of him who called you out of darkness into his wonderful light (1 Pet. 2:4–5, 9).

The question of ordaining women as priests needs to be put on hold. The first question is whether *men* should be ordained as priests! In Christ, who is our High Priest, each Christian has direct access to God without the intervention of anyone else (Heb. 4:14–16). By following Church tradition, which ordains *special* priests, we have reverted to the Mosaic Law and its inhibiting concept of priesthood. We have presumptuously placed a formally-ordained professional clergy between the believer and his or her God.

Let no one think that we are quibbling here merely about terminology. I am aware that several evangelical authors in the Church of England put forth a case for the word *priest* deriving from *presbyteros*, the Greek word for elder. Whatever we might call these special servants of God, however, priests in the Church of England are closer in function to Old Testament priests (who administered ritual offerings and rites of covenant) than New Testament elders (who fed and led the flock of God among them through word and deed). What *special* authority, for example, did first-century elders have to perform baptisms or to distribute the communion? Recapturing the Biblical concept of spiritual shepherds who exercise non-authoritative servant leadership would go a long way towards solving many of the problems now facing an entrenched hierarchy of Church officials.

If David Jenkins wants to take the Church to task for unbiblical tradition (and he should), then he must begin with his own priesthood! Even a cursory reading of the New Testament will confirm that today's idea of priesthood was not a part of first-century Christianity.

If ever we could move away from the human tradition of priesthood, we could stop arguing about who has the right to administer the sacrament of communion. If ever we could move away from the human tradition of hierarchical Church structure, we might even get away from arguing about which body has the right to make that decision. Following the Biblical pattern rather than historically-supported Church tradition would prevent most of the current questions dividing us. Locally-autonomous Church leadership would still be male, but for God's reasons, not man's. Moreover, it would have much more to do with *responsibility* for spiritual leading than what too often appears to be the maintenance of *privilege* or, worse yet, power politics.

The Blasphemy of Human Tradition

Contrary to what you may have supposed by now, I do not believe that blasphemy is to be found under every rock. Nevertheless, Church tradition can become a matter of blasphemy when it demands precedence over God's own revelation. For in the practice of tradition unsupported by Scripture is an implicit assertion that we know better than God how we ought to live and worship. When we follow Church tradition for its own sake, we are saying to God, 'We are God and you are not. We will do as we wish!' That contempt for God's will is as blasphemous as any verbal epithets which might be hurled against God by a God-hating unbeliever.

As we have seen before, the contempt of the believer is compounded all the more. From the lips of Jesus comes the warning: 'Why do you call me, "Lord, Lord," and do not do what I say?' (Luke 6:46). Jesus knew full well the danger of human tradition, and even more so its affront to God's revelation. Speaking out against the Pharisees, who had made an art-form of religious tradition, Jesus pulled no punches:

> . . . you nullify the word of God for the sake of your tradition. You hypocrites! Isaiah was right when he prophesied about you: 'These people honour me with their lips, but their hearts are far from me. They worship me in vain; their teachings are but rules taught by men' (Matt. 15:6–9).

We should think it idolatrous – and blasphemous – if others were to set up another god and look to him as their spiritual authority. Are we any less idolatrous – or blasphemous – when we look to Church history as our spiritual authority? The Apostle Paul gives us this caution regarding human tradition:

> See to it that no-one takes you captive through hollow and deceptive philosophy, which depends on human tradition and the basic principles of this world rather than on Christ (Col. 2:8).

That's the trouble with tradition. Invariably it masks our own ideas, or the world's. It lowers God's teaching to our own level, and in its presumptuousness profanes the sacred. Blasphemy is nothing new in our time. Even in the Church it has a long and time-honoured tradition.

*

Tradition's Most Serious Failure

Vaunting human tradition is not only *blasphemous*, but *impractical* as well. What's more, there is a tie between the two. When we contemptuously proceed on the basis of human thinking, we forfeit having the benefit of God's perfect knowledge. After all, because God made us, he knows how we best function. That's why he has revealed his mind to us, to give us 'manufacturer's operating instructions', if you will. When we ignore his instructions, we are bound to suffer. Inevitably, things will go awry.

Surely it doesn't take an outsider to tell anyone that Christian faith is on a downhill slide in Britain. How often I have attended Evensong in the larger Churches, only to be invited into the choir stalls because so few people are attending. As Church attendance dwindles, one house of worship after another is falling into disuse.

In their 1989 annual report, the Church Commissioners acknowledge that the Church of England alone has demolished 289 Churches and closed another 926 over the past twenty years. Many have been sold off as private homes, aerobic centres, and bedding warehouses. The commissioners said despondency among Anglicans was misplaced, but admitted that the statistics could be interpreted as symptoms of a 'Church in retreat'.

No one reason can ever safely be cited as the cause of a Church's decline, but I offer one very basic reason, simply as a graphic example of how destructive human tradition can be. The most unlikely suspect, I suggest, is the tradition of infant baptism.

Not practised by the early Church until somewhere around the end of the second century, infant baptism was unknown during the time of the Apostles. It was known at the time of Origen and Tertullian, though Tertullian opposed it on the grounds that it would be safer and more profitable to wait until faith was formed in the believing adult. Because Origen wrote that 'the Church has received a tradition from the Apostles to give baptism even to little children', it was assumed by most that the practice was in fact Biblical.

Only through the use of various theological devices (original sin or covenant theology) however, is one able to rationalise what was clearly a different practice in the apostolic Church. Adult-believing baptism was *The Normal Christian Birth*, as David Pawson puts it well in his recent book (Hodder & Stoughton, 1989).

In an issue of *Renewal* magazine last year, I noted with interest the following letter from Alan J. Wright, a Church of England vicar:

> Both now and at the time of the Reformation most of those pressing for reform were afraid to grasp the nettle of infant baptism. It was an aspect of non-Biblical Church practice that they were *not* prepared to reform. The reformers clutched at the straw of covenant theology in order to maintain an unbiblical practice that was dearly loved by the average layman and woman.
>
> The evangelical Anglican, almost to a man (and woman), gratefully continues this tradition, despite the massive Biblical evidence against it.

My point in raising the issue of infant baptism in a book on blasphemy is to show how far afield we can go when we profane the sacred pattern through human tradition, and how disastrous that 'theological blasphemy' can be. Alan Wright's further comment highlights the larger picture: 'The growth of infant baptism produced a powerless Church.'

Have we really stopped to analyse *why* the Church in England is on a slippery slope into oblivion? I suggest it is because millions of Britons are baptised but unconverted. They are baptised by proxy at a time when they know neither sin, repentance, faith, nor salvation.

'Theological Blasphemy' 139

There is no rebirth of the spirit by the Spirit. No personal persuasion. No Christian commitment. Not even the unbiblical practice of confirmation – itself invented to make up for that which is obviously missing in infant baptism – can bridge the gap for most people.

Why, then, are we surprised that we have a moribund Church? If we have steadfast believers keeping the doors of the Church open today (and we do, praise God!), it is *in spite of* their nearly-aborted birthing process. Where are all the others who were dutifully baptised as infants? Why do we have a nation filled with nominal Christians for whom Church is a place where you are baptised, confirmed, married, and buried – and little or nothing in between?

A Lesson From Muslims

I was moved to tears recently as I read *I Dared To Call Him Father* (Kingsway), by Bilquis Sheikh, a high-born Muslim woman who came to know Christ through her private reading of the Bible. In the touching story of her conversion from Islam to Christianity, she realised that baptism initiated a crucial, irreversible personal commitment to her new faith. She also knew that it was likely to bring about her death:

> Why did my heart skip at the word 'baptised?' I knew little about these Christians, but all Muslims had heard of their strange ceremony of baptism. My mind flitted to the many people who were murdered after their baptisms. And this also happened under British rule when supposedly there was freedom of religion. Even as a child I had put the two facts together: a Muslim was baptised, a Muslim died (p. 32).

Missionaries to Muslims tell of the agony they face when a Muslim finally decides to become a Christian through faith-responsive baptism. They know that in many cases they are signing the new believer's death warrant. I titled a recent book for an American audience, *Baptism – The Believer's Wedding Ceremony*. For many among a Muslim audience it would be titled more appropriately, *Baptism – The Believer's Funeral Service*.

There is a sense, of course, in which the latter would be a better title. In baptism, the believer dies to sin, is buried with Christ, and rises from his watery grave to live a new life in the Spirit. That is the picture Paul gives us in his letter to the Roman Christians:

> . . . don't you know that all of us who were baptised into Christ Jesus were baptised into his death? We were therefore buried with him through baptism into death in order that, just as Christ was raised from the dead through the glory of the Father, we too may live a new life (Rom. 6:3–4).

Perhaps more than Christians, Muslims understand the significance of Biblical baptism. It is a symbolic act of *commitment* to one's faith. Muslims can study the Bible, attend Christian worship services, and pray in the name of Christ, if they wish, with little adverse reaction from the Muslim community. By contrast, however, being baptised in Muslim nations is *the* act of apostasy. It is the fatal line of demarcation, because it is a conscious decision to put away one's past – both one's sin and any previous religious loyalties. The new Christian dies to Islam and, for many even today, must die literally at the hands of their own families.

Even here in Britain the tragic killing of a sixteen-year-old girl by her devout Muslim father is a reminder of the serious consequences which can attend anyone converting from Islam to Christianity. Abdul Malik, of

Birmingham, had warned his daughter not to consider so drastic a change in faith. When she persisted in her Christian beliefs and refused to say 'Allah', Malik pushed her to the floor in his wife's presence and slashed his daughter's throat.

The amazing thing is how many Muslims in predominantly Islamic countries are willing to turn to Christianity and to be buried with Christ in baptism, knowing that physical death could be the result. How many of us would be willing to be baptised under threat of death? For how many of us was baptism a real turning point in our lives? How is it possible that baptism of infants can *ever* be a turning point, a statement of faith, a personal commitment? No wonder, then, that so many are baptised but unconverted. No wonder that the Church collectively is tepid and languid and searching for its spiritual identity.

Ideas have consequences. Wrong ideas have disastrous consequences. 'Blasphemous theology' has disastrous *eternal* consequences. *Lord, may we cease from profaning your Word by our own traditions!*

The Awesome Responsibility of Spiritual Leadership

At this point I am reminded of Jeremiah's harsh rebuke of religious leaders who lead others astray by distorting the Scriptures:

> How can you say, 'We are wise, for we have the law of the Lord,' when actually the lying pen of the scribes has handled it falsely? The wise will be put to shame; they will be dismayed and trapped. Since they have rejected the word of the Lord, what kind of wisdom do they have? (Jer. 8:8).

The Word of God in the hands of those who lack respect

for its inviolability deprives even them of the wisdom which comes from above. It makes a mockery of revelation and of the God of revelation. Not the least, it makes a mockery of spiritual leadership to which the Church has been called.

Perhaps the most serious practical consequence which results is that those who seek spiritual guidance are led blindly into destructive paths. I do not know of a more poignant passage in all Scripture than the powerful warning from the prophet Ezekiel to the leaders of Israel who had caused the people to be led away into idolatry. Those of us who are in positions of influence in today's Church ought to read it each morning on our knees. A brief excerpt from chapter 34 will give us the flavour:

> Son of man, prophesy against the shepherds of Israel; prophesy and say to them: 'This is what the Sovereign Lord says: Woe to the shepherds of Israel who only take care of themselves! Should not shepherds take care of the flock?
>
> You have not strengthened the weak or healed the sick or bound up the injured. You have not brought back the strays or searched for the lost. You have ruled them harshly and brutally. So they were scattered because there was no shepherd, and when they were scattered they became food for all the wild animals' (Ezek. 34:2, 4–5).

With our houses of worship as empty as they are, where are the strays? Have we searched for them, to bring them back and strengthen them? Have we searched our hearts for the reasons why they left? Does it have anything to do with our own lack of spiritual shepherding? If so, God's warning through Ezekiel is addressed to us:

> This is what the Sovereign Lord says: I am against the shepherds and will hold them accountable for my flock. I will remove them from tending the flock so that the shepherds can no longer feed themselves. I will rescue my flock from their mouths, and it will no longer be food for them (Ezek. 34:10).

There is a sense in which each of us, whether a spiritual leader or a spiritual follower, is responsible for his own understanding of the will of God. Each of us needs to be engaged in the prayerful study of the Word. But those who are in positions of spiritual leadership bear the greater responsibility. It is for the shepherds to watch and to warn. It is for the leaders to take the first bold steps away from unbiblical tradition. It is for those who guide to lead the way back to New Testament Christianity.

When a failure to do that causes men and women in the pew to abandon their faith, it is the leaders whom God will hold accountable. Not the seduction of secular humanism. Not the lure of competing religions. Not the spiritual dulling of rampant materialism. A tradition-bound Church and its leaders have much for which to answer! If the Church is to be the guardian against blasphemy among an unbelieving world, who guards the *Church* from profaning the sacred?

Contempt By Ignorance

Behind the blasphemy of human tradition is the blasphemy of ignorance. I say *blasphemy* of ignorance looking to the significance of the root word *ignore*. One of the classic ways to show contempt for people is simply to ignore them, as if they are not worthy of our time and attention. As if we have no need of what they have to offer. As if we are on a higher level of existence than they. How God must feel, knowing that we do not even take the time and effort to read or reflect on his revealed Word, his divine overture of love to us all!

Human tradition does not flourish in an environment of widespread Biblical knowledge. In the light of Biblical understanding, inconsistent human tradition is all too glaring. The problem today is that most people, including a high percentage of Christians, do not know their Bibles. They don't read them, they don't study them, they don't understand them. As a result, they have no way of knowing that they are often practising *traditional* Christianity as opposed to *Biblical* Christianity. All they have ever known is a rather institutionalised, historically-validated *style* of Christianity. Unacquainted with the genuine, they can't recognise the counterfeit.

There is something terribly pernicious about a 'Christian society' in which there is an established Church that is responsible for the religious education of the vast majority of the nation's young people. An assumption seems to follow that, therefore, the vast majority of people in Britain understand what Christianity is all about. The truth is that they don't. In some respects it would be better if Britain were an avowed secularist nation. Then we could no longer proceed under the illusion of being a 'Christian nation' whose citizens are intimately familiar with the teachings of the Bible. Then we should have to redouble our efforts to teach the Scriptures and get back to basics.

As an outsider looking in, I get the feeling that parents delegate the responsibility for teaching their children about the Bible to the Church, which delegates it to the school system, which delegates it to individual teachers, whose parents delegated it to the Church . . . and so on. Is that too harsh a judgment? What other explanation is there for the Biblical illiteracy which abounds?

The last thing anyone in this country wants is to have a critical American observer compare religion in Britain with religion in America. From your outsider's perspective of our own problems, you will be wanting to say, 'Physician, heal thyself!' Yet despite its own increase in Biblical illiteracy over the past two decades, the Christian community in America contains a substantial segment of people who know their Bibles.

The reason is hardly a secret. They *read* their Bibles and *study* their Bibles. Significant numbers read the Bible as part of a daily routine. Many more attend Sunday School classes in their churches, and that includes adults as well as children. In many major Christian fellowships, the quest for Biblical knowledge is a lifetime pursuit. By contrast, I am amazed at the almost total absence of Church-sponsored Bible study in this country.

Perhaps this brings us back to the different venues of Biblical learning. Whereas, in Britain, religious instruction is part of a broader educational instruction within the school system, in America (for Constitutional reasons) we don't even allow the Lord's Prayer to be recited. 'Religious education' is something which takes place in the home and in the Church.

The difference is crucial. A school system in a pluralistic society must be all things to all people — which, unfortunately, means that the instruction must be watered down and understated. It seldom goes beyond the level of ancient history and generalised moral virtues. In a church setting, by contrast, even sin and salvation become legitimate topics for instruction, by people who are interested in spirituality as well as historical detail.

Maybe he doesn't speak for everyone, or even a majority, but my barber recently expressed a sentiment which certainly would make sense for most people taking *any* required subject in school. 'They crammed religious training down our throats,' he said (by way of justifying why he never took a serious interest in religion). No wonder few people are keen to study the Bible for themselves once they have managed to survive their A-levels.

Nowadays, it is almost futile to expect unknowledgeable (if not unbelieving) parents to teach the Bible to their children in the home. Therefore, the Church must rise to the challenge of Biblical education, both for young people and adults. Failure to do so will leave us in a position of contempt against God and his revelation for our lives. As in the days of Hosea, the summons for that contempt will be placed in the hands of those who lead the Church as well as in the hands of the rest of us:

> My people are destroyed from lack of knowledge. Because you have rejected knowledge, I also reject you as my priests; because you have ignored the law of your God, I also will ignore your children. The more the priests increased, the more they sinned against me; they exchanged their Glory for something disgraceful. They feed on the sins of my people and relish their wickedness. And it will be: Like people, like priests. I will punish both of them for their ways and repay them for their deeds (Hosea 4:6–9).

Obviously, Britain is not the first nation to suffer from a lack of spiritual knowledge, but we can hardly take comfort in that. The 'blasphemy of ignorance', which leads in turn to 'theological blasphemy', is cause for the gravest possible concern. Whether it be questions about the role of women in the Church, or the nature of the priesthood in the kingdom of Christ, or the nature and form of Christian baptism, we must carefully distinguish between Biblical authority and human tradition. Yet how shall we be able to make that distinction unless we open our Bibles and get back into the Word!

11

Sacrilege By Saints

Confusing the Secular and the Sacred

> It were better to have no opinion of God at all than such a one as is unworthy of him; for the one is only unbelief – the other is contempt.
>
> Plutarch

Some years ago, I was driving randomly through southern New England on a holiday, not intending any particular destination for the night. As it happened, I ended up near New Haven, Connecticut, and decided to try and see a friend of mine who teaches there at Yale Divinity School. When a phone call to his home got no answer, I drove to the campus in the hope that I might find him working late at his office.

At first the school seemed totally abandoned. Even the library was deserted. Hearing some commotion in the distance, however, I followed the sound to its source, a large hall filled with students and faculty. No one noticed my entry, because they were rocking with laughter at a presentation taking place on a make-shift stage. I soon gathered it was a sort of graduation party, with skits and poems and other reminiscences of the past school year.

It wasn't long before this large group of divinity students and their theologian professors (my friend was absent, for whatever reason) were roaring with howls of approval at one particular skit which made me very uncomfortable. A student wearing clerical robes and other religious regalia was putting on a mock eucharist ceremony. Every line was a double-entendre calculated to poke fun at the distribution of the sacred emblems of communion. Eventually, he put grapes into an electric food blender to make the 'wine', and he threw hastily-torn pieces of Wonder Bread (a white, soft, doughy American product) into the screaming audience. They, in turn, cheered as they grabbed their pieces of bread and put them gleefully into their mouths.

It was one of those occasions when you had to be there in order to appreciate what was happening. However, I can tell you that few people would not have judged it to be highly sacrilegious. I went away not only disappointed in having missed my friend, but greatly distressed at what I had witnessed from people who one day would be leaders within the Christian community. For days, I couldn't get the picture of their sacrilege out of my mind. Was it not blasphemy in the eyes of God?

A Matter of Sacrilege

Discussion of sacrilege is conspicuously absent from the literature dealing with legal blasphemy. One would have thought the two concepts go hand in glove. Yet perhaps there is this difference: compared with legal blasphemy, which focuses on the misuse of words, sacrilege (outside any legal context) is the misuse or desecration of anything regarded as sacred. Possibly it could be said that sacrilege is an umbrella term inclusive of blasphemy.

We get a better idea of sacrilege when we see the breadth with which it can be used. For example, there is the controversy in Russia over the possible removal of Lenin's body from Moscow's Red Square to a less public site. Right in the heart of an officially atheistic nation, you hear such religious terminology as 'shrine' and 'pilgrimage' used in connection with Lenin's tomb. Interestingly, Lenin's niece, Olga Ulyanova, in an interview with the orthodox daily newspaper *Sovietskaya Rossiya*, even uses the word *sacrilege* when objecting to disturbing Lenin's remains.

Xan Smiley reports from Moscow that the stir has been caused by Moscow radicals who have suggested that 'the holy shrine of Bolshevik communism has become an outdated symbol, with religious overtones that Lenin himself would have scorned'. Even in the Soviet Union, one person's glasnost is another's blasphemy.

Another example of sacrilege is found in the hapless burial of the Ayatollah Khomeini. I don't know the Arabic equivalent of 'sacrilege' or whether it was used to describe what happened, but when the frenzied mobs mourning the Ayatollah's death irreverently tipped his body on to the ground and tore off pieces of his shroud, it could have been nothing less than sacrilege within the context of Islam. (Something like the Roman soldiers at the foot of the cross profaning our Saviour by putting his clothes to a lottery.)

The sacrilege was all the more ironic, considering that one of the most vicious curses for Shi'ite Muslims says, 'May you be buried in a torn shroud!' Further compounding the offence, the stolen pieces of shroud were put in plastic sachets and offered for sale at up to £30 apiece in the Tehran bazaar.

Sacrilege, then, is the idea of turning something that ought to be holy or sacred or respected into something which is not. In a *secular* sense, sacrilege may be almost any form of desecration (as in burning a country's flag in a political protest), or inappropriateness (as in holding a party in a cemetery), or, at its lowest level, merely violating a given society's 'sacred cows' (as in removing one's jacket on a hot day at Henley!).

The more important sacrilege, pertaining to that which is *holy* or *sacred*, may be making light of Biblical personages, as when the BBC programme *Something For the Weekend* (June 17th, 1989) showed Abraham covering the face of Isaac with custard pie while the Twenty-third Psalm was being sung. It is the failure to recognise that even humour has its limits, that mixture of the sacred and the secular is a precarious balance indeed.

Christ and Sacrilege

A good example of sacrilege is found in the Bible, where Jesus himself drew the ire of the Pharisees when his disciples picked grain in the fields and ate it on the Sabbath, a holy day, a day for honouring the sacred by suspending all 'work' (Matt. 12:1–8). In order to emphasise the importance of human needs, Jesus referred to an occasion centuries earlier involving Israel's King David and his companions. In need of food, they entered the house of God and ate the consecrated bread – which was not lawful for them to do, only for the priests.

Jesus's reference to David's use of the sacred bread for a profane, non-sacred purpose is an instance where the exception proves the rule. Jesus was not urging sacrilege, but the proper ordering of spiritual priorities. We can commit sacrilege, then, when we elevate even religious exercise over obvious and immediate needs of our fellow man.

Jesus turned the tables on his critics (that is, *overturned* them) when he cleansed the outer court of the Temple after it had been converted from a house of worship into an entrepreneurial enterprise. Look at the contrast which he makes between the holy and the profane:

> Jesus entered the temple area and drove out all who were buying and selling there. He overturned the tables of the money changers and the benches of those selling doves. 'It is written,' he said to them, '"My house will be called a house of prayer," but you are making it a "den of robbers"' (Matt. 21:12–13).

One wonders how Jesus might feel about the souvenir vendors in today's 'houses of prayer'. Yet they probably are among the least of his concerns, given the many other ways in which we misuse the holy for secular purposes.

The Church: Building or People?

From the locals, my American accent invariably evokes a question about what I am doing in England for months at a time each year. When I respond that I am a writer, inevitably the eyes light up. 'Novels?' they ask hopefully. By now I anticipate the disappointment that will register on their faces when I say it's Christian books that I write. (I realise the least I could do is to say that I write books on gardening or sport, the nation's *other* religions.)

The second reaction that I now anticipate is a half-embarrassed, half-proud reference to the local church, as if that might interest a writer of Christian books – also, as if the village church somehow bridges the gap between a Christian writer and a non-churchgoer. Of course, I suspect that I return the disappointment when I don't always rush off to view the beautiful stained glass or glistening church spire.

I wince at the thought that, for millions of people, 'the church' means nothing more than stained glass and steeples. When I think of 'the church' I think of the *congregation*. That is the only way that the Bible ever speaks of the Church – as the body of believers in Christ, whether universally or locally. Don't get me wrong, I don't propose that it is sinful to refer to the spired building in the centre of the village as 'the church'. What is dismaying is the fact that, for so many people, that is *all* that the Church means.

In this regard I am fortunate to be part of a church fellowship which happens to have no building whatever of its own. The University Church, which meets on the campus of the university where I teach, currently worships in one of the school's auditoriums. It's a nice reminder of the Church as *family* rather than the church as *building*.

A Church in Ruins

It is bad enough when those in the secular world cannot distinguish between the building itself and the body which uses the building. Worse still, it approaches sacrilege when not even the Church can distinguish between itself and the building in which it meets for worship. It becomes sacrilege when the building receives as much attention as the souls of the people who seek its hallowed walls in quest of a relationship with God.

One will have to decide for himself as to how much attention is given respectively to buildings and people. It probably varies from place to place. I simply raise

Sacrilege By Saints

the issue so that we can check our own practice in a vulnerable area.

What comes immediately to mind, of course, are the many fund-raising appeals for the maintenance of Britain's ancient cathedrals. Sensitive as I am to the concern for these irreplaceable works of architecture, I cannot help but wonder how the Church would grow if we had anywhere near the concern for the lost souls in Hereford, or in York, or in Canterbury. (Is even the phrase 'lost souls' shocking in these modern times?) Are we worried more about the roofs falling in on our ageing churches than we are about the salvation of those who, for lack of Christian faith, have never sat beneath them?

I can't tell you how very much I admire the two couples in my village who get out each week and take care of the lawn in the churchyard and cemetery. Theirs is truly a labour of love. Last week I joined them to remove grass and weeds from along the old stone wall between the church and the road. It had been many years since the walls were so beautifully exposed to all who pass by. At day's end, we stood back and admired the fruits of our efforts, thrilled with the sense of timelessness that the old wall added to our already charming little village.

I couldn't help but imagine the people of faith centuries before who had built the village church and, with great effort, laid the stones in that wall. What it must have been like in a time when churches sprang up in every village and dale across this nation! When churches were filled to overflowing. When the bells rang out and people actually came to worship. When the church was a way of life. How very far we have come from those days!

Now we hardly muster a quorum. We find it difficult even to maintain the buildings once so grandly built in an age of faith. Now we turn to village fêtes, raffles, and jumble sales to try and put things right.

I am sympathetic with Eastbourne's vicar, John Harrington, who told his parishioners at St Michael and All Angels, 'We shall not beg, neither shall we turn the church into a den of thieves.' He went on to explain his 'great feeling of disquiet about raising money through a constant string of jumble sales and bring-and-buys.' Like his Saviour before him, the vicar was rightly concerned about sacrilege in sacred causes:

> When faced with enormous sums of money we find it is easy to panic and start organising all the usual churchy activities and ways of begging from the non-church-going public.
> But it is our problem and we shall not beg, neither shall we turn the church into a den of thieves.

Then the vicar touched the sensitive nerve of this book, saying he hoped that other churches still influenced by the 'jumble-sale mentality' would 'look at what we are doing and realise that such activities are *unworthy* of God and the Church'.

Sacrilege of the Unworthy

What a wonderful way to describe sacrilege: *Unworthy*! When I think of all the time, effort and money spent on the upkeep of Britain's houses of worship (£48 million needed for cathedral repairs in *one* year alone!), and how little time, effort and money is spent in sharing Christ with those without faith, I shudder at how *unworthy* our Christian faith has become. I like to think that I am as proud of Britain's cathedrals, abbeys and village churches as are the British people themselves. I hate to see any of them fall into disrepair. However, if we were given a choice between our church buildings falling down and the people of this nation being spiritually edified, then let the buildings fall! All of them. Down to St Paul's itself, if necessary!

Anthony Burgess reminds us that 'York Minster was struck by secular lightning and £3 million has been spent on the restoration of a masterpiece of medieval art rather than a centre of worship.' Considering the way we often refer to natural disasters, others have suggested that the lightning in this case was *truly* 'an act of God'.

Could it be that God himself is causing the roofs to fall in and the walls to crumble? Is he trying to get our attention – to keep us from confusing bricks and mortar with the 'living stones' he has called us to be? Maybe it's God's way of cleansing the Temple all over again. Who knows? When the last building has fallen, perhaps we shall be forced to meet from house to house, where there is intimate sharing and caring. Where Christian fellowship becomes like family. Where the offering is not for bricks but for bread for the needy. Where stained-glass windows are replaced by blood-stained believers. Where instead of steeples pointing heavenward, holy lives are pointing to Christ. Where Christian worship is *worthy* of the God of Creation!

There is a wonderful passage in the letter to the Hebrews that humbles me every time I read it. It speaks of those great heroes of faith who would have found our dilapidated buildings a luxury. In the midst of jumble-sale sacrilege, it rings out shame to us all.

> [They] were tortured and refused to be released, so that they might gain a better resurrection. Some faced jeers and flogging, while still others were chained and put in prison. They were stoned; they were sawn in two; they were put to death by the sword. They went about in sheepskins and goatskins, destitute, persecuted and ill-treated . . . They wandered in deserts

and mountains, and in caves and holes in the ground (Heb. 11:35–8).

What would these heroes of faith think of our building fund appeals and jumble sales? What would they think of us, sitting in our finely restored buildings, going through the motions of repetitious ritual week after week, year after year, with little personal spiritual growth and no compelling concern for Christian evangelism?

I purposely omitted from the passage above one of the most moving epitaphs of all time. It deserves a solo appearance. Any less attention would itself be a sacrilege. Bestowing uncommon honour, the inspired author wrote simply, 'The world was not worthy of them.' The world was not *worthy*!

Unlike too many of us, they had a keen sense of the sacred. Unlike today's Church, they had a correctly prioritised sense of values. Sacrifice for them did not mean dipping into one's bank account to support the local building fund. It meant sharing their faith at the risk of their lives! It meant calling an unappreciative world to righteousness, even in the face of ridicule and persecution. They *recognised* that which was worthy. They *proclaimed* that which was worthy. They *lived* that which was worthy.

Do we recognise, proclaim and live that which is worthy? Or have we cheapened it all with that which is *un*worthy? Which is closer to our experience – genuine saintliness or counterfeit sacrilege?

Sacrilege by Diluting the Sacred

I find myself turning time and again to Anthony Burgess's insightful and urgent message (*Sunday Times Magazine*, December 24th, 1988) in which he asks the tough question, 'What Happened to Christianity?' It ought to be required reading among the Christian community. He has seen a trend in the Roman Catholic Church wherein that which has been considered sacred has been cheapened in the name of modern progressiveness:

> The liberalisation of Church ritual meant chiefly its vulgarisation – louts with guitars moaning pop-songs about God's love, inept choreography, new ecumenical prayers in tired English. And the way was open for the conflation of Marxism and Christianity.

The greater harm, of course, has come from doctrinal liberalism, to which vernacular worship takes a back seat. Yet even in evangelical Christian circles, we have encountered what I should call Christian fluff. Touchy-feely stuff, with just that right combination of shallowness and entertainment value. Oh, I don't blame anyone for running kicking and screaming away from dry, cold, unmoving High Church ritual. Each extreme can make the other look good. Yet at least with most ritual there is a feeling that God is held in awe. If turning to a more experiential expression of faith has its virtues, it also threatens to cheapen the message.

Again, Burgess calls the right number:

> What people clearly don't want is the terrible message of Christianity, which enjoins an acceptance of the God-man as a daily presence and an approach to daily conduct which entails salvation and damnation. In Britain at least we might as well write Christianity off. It's either bigoted (with the Lord Chancellor condemned for attending a Catholic mass) or gentlemanly and tepid. Christ said he'd vomit the lukewarm out of his mouth.

Sacrilege occurs when we pick only the good parts of Christianity and ignore the parts we don't want to face, Heaven is fine for the once-a-week Christian, but hell has no place. Homilies from the pulpit warm our hearts, but hard preaching on moral issues drives a few people away. Knowing that, the Church has often preached a gospel of accommodation on issues such as homosexuality and abortion.

William Westwood, Bishop of Peterborough, is disturbed that the Church is *intellectually* rather than *spiritually* driven, and he minces no words:

> Intellectual priests are given to the subordinate clause and the conditional mood – on the one hand and on the other – and in the Church of England the passive voice and the conditional mood have largely displaced the active voice and totally displaced the imperative.

In an interview with Graham Turner (*Sunday Telegraph*, March 26th, 1989), Westwood pressed his point as it related to practising homosexuals in the pulpit.

> His own view was that a man who engaged in homosexual activity ought not to be exercising ministry, full stop. A lot of bishops, however, being intellectually directed, didn't want to seem narrow-minded, so there was a dither. They didn't want to upset a minority, but they were perfectly prepared to upset the heterosexual majority, who were then accused of homophobia.
>
> As for calling homosexuality a sin, Westwood went on, they certainly were not going to risk that. After all, you might get the definition of sin wrong, so it was better not to try.

Sacrilege By Saints

What can be more of an affront to God than calling sin 'no sin'! What can be more of a sacrilege of the sacredness of marriage than to put the Church's stamp of approval on homosexual relationships? How more could we blaspheme the Word of God!

Trading Politics for Salvation

If the Church is speaking with increasing uncertainty in the realm of morality and religion, it is speaking with increasing certainty in the realm of politics. My suggestion that this, too, is a profaning of the greater spiritual calling of the Church is likely to be met by references to the call of the ancient prophets for social justice. Or perhaps I'll be directed to Jesus's repeated condemnation of abstract religiosity which fails to meet the needs of a suffering world. Naturally, I agree that religion confined to the pew is empty religion. The Gospel concerns both salvation and social justice.

In his letter defining true religion for first-century believers, James merged the parallel spiritual and social obligations of the Christian:

> Religion that God our Father accepts as pure and faultless is this: to look after orphans and widows in their distress and to keep oneself from being polluted by the world (Jas. 1:27).

Unable to agree on how to keep us unpolluted by the world, Church leaders have opted for the arguably-easier Christian duty of social involvement. In fact, they have gone beyond the Biblical call for social involvement by individual Christians lending a helping hand where needed. They have dared to enter the arena of politics as an institutional force like any other trade union, or business lobby, or political party.

You see this involvement not only from the Church of England, which has natural, constitutional ties with government and politics, but from other churches as well. One of the more glaring examples, of course, is the recent castigation of the government by Dr John Vincent, head of the British Methodist Church. He said, 'Current policies are a betrayal of [Christian] tradition. They are not, as some claim, Christian tradition, but a perversion of it.'

In what surely must be an incongruous mixture of Christian belief and atheistic social economics, Dr Vincent wrote a 'Christian' version of the Red Flag for the Methodist Conference. The chorus included this line: 'We'll keep Christ's red flag flying here.' God may not be a Tory . . . but a *Marxist*?

Forget the sacrilege of confused priorities, for the moment. Surely religious leaders must see that such political action involves them with the very political institutions which they condemn for sticking their collective nose into religious affairs! Surely they have learned the lesson of Islamic mullahs interfering with government, where what was achieved was a religious brand of politics rather than a holy nation!

Are Church leaders ready to align themselves with a socially-conscious political party whose leader is an avowed atheist, and who, if Prime Minister, would be in the curious position of appointing bishops and archbishops such as themselves? On the other hand, are Church leaders content to support a political party which talks a good deal about conservative morality, but, at least to many, lacks social concern?

Where the Labour leader seems to think that Christian ethics can exist independently of Christian faith, the Conservative leader appears to believe that nominal Christian faith automatically produces Christian ethics. Both are seriously wrong.

*

Sacrilege By Saints   161

Is There a 'Christian Party Platform'?

One might ask, from what source are the politics of the Church to be derived? Certainly, the Bible calls for social justice, but is that necessarily to come through the Labour Party's platform? God created man to rule over the earth as a good steward, but does that mean we must vote 'Green' in Euro-parliamentary elections? In other words, how are we to know – as Christians – that we have a divine mandate for political action in any particular direction?

I wonder if Mr Kenneth Baker isn't right in saying that political or social assertions made by Churchmen should be clearly derived from Christian doctrine and 'not just from a fashionable analysis of contemporary views'.

A case in point is the Church of England's support for disinvestment and sanctions against South Africa. A little-heralded meeting took place not long ago between the Bishop of Coventry and two black Church leaders from South Africa. They had come on an improbable mission: to persuade the Church to reverse its stand on sanctions. 'It is destroying our black families,' said one of the visitors. 'When I talk of a family, I'm talking of a man with no less than seven mouths to feed. When he loses his job because of sanctions, his dignity is pulled to the ground. Anger breeds within him.' A sensible enough argument, so it seems. Even one backed by Christian concern for those who suffer.

However, columnist Barbara Amiel, who attended the meeting, reported a chilly reception for such concern by the chairman of the International Affairs Division of the Board of Social Responsibility of the Church of England. (His title alone ought to tell us how far over the top the Church has gone!) According to Amiel (*The Times*, April 21st, 1989), the Bishop didn't want to hear the result of polls indicating that the majority of blacks in South

Africa did not support sanctions or disinvestment. The visitors were soon on their way with little more to show for their 4,000-mile journey than a hollow handshake.

Amiel's conclusion did not put the Church or Christianity in the best possible light:

> The meeting was the laboratory proof of one's fear that the Church of England is in the grip of a certain world view and will not endanger it by the uncertainties of an open mind.
>
> For reasons that were never specified or that are anybody's guess, every question the black bishops had as to why the Church of England was pursuing its pro-ANC policies remained unanswered.

The issue is not whether sanctions are the best solution to the problem of apartheid. Nor whether the Bishop of Coventry was closed-minded in summarily dismissing the views of his South African visitors. The issue is whether a Biblical mandate against racial injustice necessarily leads Christians to the conclusion that sanctions are the best way to achieve the desired end. Whether there is something in Scripture that would compel *all* Christians to take that particular political position. Whether it would be a sin to disagree on the methods to be used in bringing an end to apartheid.

Nothing in Scripture suggests that there is such a thing as *the* Christian view on every political issue that comes along. Did Jesus tell us what we ought to think about the community charge or poll tax? Did he condemn it as immoral? Certainly the Apostolic letters give us no specific instructions as to how we are to deal with the homeless. Nor are we told whether nuclear weapons are morally different in kind from non-nuclear weapons designed to kill our fellow humans. And as much as we might desire his insight on the matter, the Apostle Paul tells us nothing about the issue of water privatisation.

Sacrilege By Saints

The answer to all of those questions is that the Bible is not a political platform. Although it calls for social concern, it does not involve the Church as an institution in political action. Are we to presume that governments today are any more corrupt or abusive than the Roman government? Yet Jesus never once took on the Roman government to press for political reforms. To the contrary, he urged submission. He told his followers to 'Give to Caesar what is Caesar's', presumably aware that a large portion of their tax money would go to support the Roman military establishment.

If scripted by the Church today, the Great Commission given to the Apostles might well have read: 'Go into all the world and get involved in politics, solving compelling social issues as you see fit to solve them.' However, that is not the way Christ scripted it. His own commission was spiritual in nature: 'Go and make disciples of all nations, baptising them in the name of the Father and of the Son and of the Holy Spirit, and teaching them to obey everything I have commanded you' (Matt. 28: 19–20).

Nor did the Apostle Paul set the liberation of slaves as his first priority. His first priority was teaching masters and slaves how to treat each other in love, whatever station they might have in life. That's not to say that Paul would have been unconcerned about apartheid in South Africa today, or about earlier times of slavery here in England, America and the West Indies. In fact, Paul includes *slave traders* in the same list of sinners as *murderers* (1 Tim. 1:9, 10). Yet Paul knew that eternal salvation in heaven was even more critical than social justice in this world. One might paraphrase Jesus: 'If the Church solves the whole world's political and social problems, but doesn't bring them into a relationship with God through Christ, what does it profit them?'

Some would contend, I think with good reason, that the Christian's task is not so much to defend the sacred, as such, but to advance the Gospel. Furthermore, that too much of an emphasis on the sacred does not sit well with an attempt to restore the radical distinctiveness of Christianity. Yet I suggest that we cannot truly advance the Gospel without defending the sacredness of the cause.

Certainly a church without social concern has badly missed the message of Christ. ('The Sabbath was made for man, not man for the Sabbath.') But if 'advancing the Gospel' means social programmes without spiritual concerns, then we have advanced the wrong 'good news'. ('What good is it for a man to gain the whole world, yet forfeit his soul?')

A second look at Jesus's own ministry reveals that, ultimately, he was more concerned about one's spiritual salvation than even the fact that one might be homeless or poor. His perfect mixture of sacred and secular concerns is perhaps best seen when he assumed the mantle of the Messiah about whom the prophet Isaiah had prophesied (Isa. 61:1, 2):

> 'The Spirit of the Lord is on me, because he has anointed me to preach good news to the poor. He has sent me to proclaim freedom for the prisoners and recovery of sight for the blind, to release the oppressed, to proclaim the year of the Lord's favour' (Luke 4:18–19).

His task, as is our own, was to feed the poor, both physically and spiritually, both body and soul. To proclaim a freedom far surpassing the concern we ought to have for those wrongly suffering imprisonment – a spiritual freedom in Christ that can nurture them even while they are still behind bars. To bring insight and understanding about eternal life, even while we do all that we can to heal those who are handicapped by blindness in this present life.

Advancing the Gospel must not be divorced from defending the sacred. The former proceeds from the latter. The latter gives reason for the former.

Recognising the Spiritual Priorities

There is much concern today that Britain's ageing infrastructure is perilously near collapse. Roads, sewers and other critical services are legitimate objects of major overhaul. Yet it is the decay of Britain's *moral* infrastructure that is most in need of attention. The writer of the proverb said it well: 'Righteousness exalts a nation, but sin is a disgrace to any people' (Prov. 14:34).

It is here that we find the critical task of the Church, which is the moral and spiritual reconstruction of the nation. Even as between the two, *spiritual* renewal is the greater priority. Only a nation which is spiritually strong can retake the moral high ground.

Political action is not God's way to change the world. It's *changed lives* that will change the world, and it is the *Word of God* that will change lives. Only a proper vertical relationship with God – salvation from sin and renewal of the spirit – can ultimately compel a proper horizontal relationship with one's fellow man. 'Liberation theology' must start with liberation from sin and guilt and self-will. Who, then, but the Church is in a position to bring the news of that liberation to a sinful world?

A Church with a political agenda debases its unique spiritual responsibility before God. It prostitutes its purpose. It turns its charter upside-down. Politics is important, but by no means sacred. In the battle for faith, we've been too long on the wrong end of the pitch. Concerted political involvement by the Church is an own goal!

The political church is engaged in backdoor theology. It is a church which attempts to heal the superficial symptoms without addressing the spiritual causes at the root of the problem. It is a church with a short-range agenda, a church which misunderstands its mission. Its mission is to bring people into a relationship with God, and into a fellowship of believers who will then go out into a world of injustice and make a difference. If step one is ignored, step two will be contrived and short-lived.

Politics is all about power. Christian faith is all about submission. Power and submission don't mix. How easily we see the truth of it in the Arab world, which has set itself on a course of political and military power while claiming allegiance to 'Islam', which very word means *submission*. If we can see the conflict between power and submission in the Muslim world, why can't we see it even more forcefully in a Christian nation?

There is yet another distinction. Where politics is about *human* power, Christian faith is all about the power of *the Holy Spirit*. Whereas political power is restricted to the limitations of human achievement, *spiritual* power through the Creator of the universe has no limits. Party politics pulls the plug on our access to God's omnipotence. When shall we learn that our Lord's Kingdom is not of this world? Ours is a greater responsibility, with a greater power. It is time that we were about our Father's business!

Cause For Disestablishment

Party politics is but the tip of the iceberg when it comes to mixing the secular and the sacred within a constitutional framework. Jesus's revolutionary separation of obligations to Caesar and to God ('Give to Caesar what is Caesar's, and to God what is God's' [Matt. 22:21]), was an implied separation between Church and state. Not that *religion* and state have nothing in common (a misguided notion wreaking moral and spiritual havoc in America), but that the *Church* is not to be encumbered by involvement in the institutionalised functioning of *government*. Why, for example, should the issue of ordination for women or for those who are divorced be a matter of public *legislation*, whatever one's views of those issues? Can you imagine how repugnant that political interference must be to Christ – to see his spiritual body, the Church, held hostage by Parliament, a secular body? Even when Parliament acts more responsibly than the Church (as in the Church's aborted attempt to ordain divorcees), it lacks divine mandate.

When shall we come to appreciate that Jesus did not (as he could have) establish a political government on earth? (*'My Kingdom is not of this earth!'*) When shall we recognise that secular government and the Church of Jesus Christ are, as Charles Colson puts it in the title of his compelling book, *Kingdoms In Conflict*? The call for Christians in Britain is not to an established *Church*, but to an established *Kingdom*! Integration of *Church* and *state* has too often meant separation of *state* and *faith*!

Secularising the sacred by the failure to separate Church and state is the ongoing stumbling-block to Christian faith in Britain. If we could ever muster enough courage to let go of the security blanket of establishment, we should find ourselves in the enviable position of *demonstrating* Christianity rather than *dictating* Christianity to a nation longing for faith but not willing to have it crammed down their throats!

Whether, then, we confuse man-made houses of worship with the spiritual body of believers on earth; or worry more about restoring crumbling church walls than restoring the dilapidated faith of an entire nation; or denigrate the mission of evangelism through power politics and a governmentally-enmeshed established Church – we profane our sacred calling. And profaning the sacred is sacrilege.

For the Church to do it is blasphemy.

12

'New Age' Blasphemy

Insidious Blasphemy Headed Our Direction

> Turn yourself into a god and then you won't have to look for another.
>
> Jane's Father
> *Tarzan the Ape Man*

For over three years now I have spent a substantial part of my time writing and speaking against the New Age Movement, the fastest growing belief system in America. It is an eclectic blend of Hinduism, Buddhism, psychic phenomena, me-generation selfism, reincarnation, and – incredibly enough – Christianity! Despite its many 'Christian' trappings, the New Age Movement is nothing short of neo-paganism, in which the highest form of idolatry is the worship of self as God.

For any Muslim readers, the New Age Movement is the West's answer to the Sufi brotherhoods, which comprise from one-third to one-half of the Muslim world. Sufis represent a more mystical dimension of Islam. Although some Sufis claim to be only the *ilhamiyya* or 'inspired of God', others boldly assert that they are *ittihadiyyah* or 'in union with God'. The latter would feel comfortable with many of the practices of the New Age Movement, including chanting, meditation and yoga. Their belief in the soul's union with the universe would also fit nicely with the New Age belief in monism – that is, that all is one, including ourselves and God.

The wonder of it all is that Sufis are not sentenced to death for apostasy. Salman Rushdie may have called into question the origins of the Qur'an, but significant segments of the Sufis go so far as to proclaim, *'Ana al haqq'*, which means 'I am the truth'! (Of course, Jesus had long before laid exclusive claim to those words: *'Ana huwa Sirat, al-haqq, al-hayat*, I am the way and the truth and the life' [John 14:6].)

Perhaps the years have brought a truce between the Sufis and other Muslims. In 922, Al-Hallaj was executed for his ideas linking man in union with God. Interestingly enough, his words could have been taken verbatim from almost any piece of New Age literature: 'I am He whom I love, and He whom I love is me.'

The most alarming aspect of the New Age Movement is that it is being accepted, supposedly with Biblical support, by bright, well-educated people in America's upper middle class. The message has a pernicious progression from 'You are God', to 'Therefore your truth is as valid as everyone else's truth', to 'Hence, there is no right; there is no wrong'! In a book of this nature, it is difficult not to anticipate what may be the most openly shameless of all blasphemies, dangerously poised for an assault on Britain.

If the New Age Movement has yet to make its mark on Britain, it will come – like 'crack' in the drug culture – with a vengeance. I predict that it may have an even greater impact in England and Europe than in the United States, for the very reasons we have been discussing. Vacuums beg to be filled. The spiritual vacuum created by the dying influence of Christianity in Britain is an open invitation to the New Age Movement, with its unique brand of relative moral values and judgment-free spirituality.

Early Signs in Britain

Already in Britain we see the first signs of the New Age culture. What tabloid today would be complete without its horoscope written by a resident psychic? Similarly, who ever could have predicted the widespread acceptability of Eastern acupuncture and psychic healing? Although these social phenomena are only on the fringe of the New Age Movement, they foreshadow the more serious assault yet to arrive.

Typical of more to come is the July 30th, 1989 issue of the *Observer In London*, presented as the 'New Age Issue', complete with articles on 'Magical, Mystical Crystals', New Age music, and a feature interview with visionary and Wrekin Trust founder Sir George Trevelyan, called 'the father of the New Age'. Says the *Observer*: 'He believes that our souls choose their incarnations. The children of today . . . will know the second coming of Christ: though not as Jesus of Nazareth marching along in a white robe. "It's the rising of love in the human heart," exclaimed Sir George, beaming with the light of which he speaks.'

Who also would have guessed a decade ago that BBC's own Radio 2 would be including among its broadcasts, programmes dedicated to astrology and dream interpretation? Or that Radio 4 would feature a lecture by Benedictine monk Bede Griffith, recorded at the Saccidananda Ashram, telling us how compatible the various world religions are and how we can achieve union with God. ('We have to recognise that God himself, the ultimate Reality, whatever name we give to it, has properly no name.')

'New Age' Blasphemy 171

Thinking of how people are now attempting a synthesis of all religions, I am reminded of the comment about God's people who had turned to idolatry: 'They spoke about the God of Jerusalem as they did about the gods of the other peoples of the world – the work of men's hands' (2 Chr. 32:19).

I need only go to my local cystic fibrosis fundraising event to be reminded of how catching is the idea that all the world's great religions are not only compatible but given to us by God in order to introduce us to the 'various facets of the divine diamond'. One of the organisers of the event, a terribly bright, well-educated and thoughtful woman, discussed with me for over an hour the easy mixture of Eastern and Western religions and the new awareness that it had brought into her life. She talked of how the various religions align perfectly with the body's chakra centres, and how she could ask questions and get answers from the vibrations on her fingertips.

I wondered to myself how she could believe that the 'divinity within us' could give her ready answers at her fingertips about life and its meaning, but apparently could not give us ready answers about cystic fibrosis and how to cure or prevent it. I also wondered, this time aloud, how she could put Jesus the Christ on a par with Buddha, Muhammad and Krishna, and yet say with complete sincerity, 'I am as Christian as anyone.' The more disquieting concern, of course, is just how long we have before her New-Age-type beliefs float down from Britain's upper-crust spiritual seekers to those who teach Britain's school-children. When it finally does happen, 'Religious Education' is going to take on a whole new meaning.

Apparently, significant inroads into the Church itself already are being made. According to Clifford Hill, editor of *Prophecy Today*, New Age services are taking place at St James's, Piccadilly. Quoting from publicity material handed out by organisers of a meditation service last

April, Hill notes that it was a celebration of 'Wesak, the full moon when the sun is in Taurus', said to be the most spiritual event of the year. The more sinister bit followed:

> This particular full moon is celebrated in the East as the Buddha's birthday. There is also a living legend that states that at this full moon the Buddha and the Christ join together with all other liberated beings and with the communion of saints to invoke a great annual blessing for the planet.

Donald Reeves, Rector of St James's, who has introduced various Eastern activities, such as yoga and holistic healing, responded adamantly to Hill's charges:

> I'm fed up with receiving letters from these sorts of people saying Jesus Christ is the sole saviour, the sole mediator.

One wonders how fed up Donald Reeves is with Jesus's assertion: 'I am the way and the truth and the life. No-one comes to the Father except through me' (John 14:6)! Putting Jesus on a par with Buddha and Krishna is a favourite plank in the New Age platform. If Jesus can be dethroned as the exclusive Son of God, then we *all* can be God! New Age is a tailor-made blasphemy!

Shirley MacLaine, Goddess of Blasphemy

My first involvement in opposition to this new belief system came in the writing of a response to actress Shirley MacLaine whose best-selling book, *Out on a Limb*, has influenced millions of people to join the Movement. My response, *Out on a Broken Limb*, led me undercover to past-life-incarnation sessions from

MacLaine's own psychic channeller, Kevin Ryerson, and to one of Shirley's own 'Getting In Touch With Your Higher Self' seminars.

To give you some feel of how popular the movement is in the States, and of the role that Ms MacLaine is playing, let me just say that, at $300 a person, there were eight hundred people at the seminar I attended. Moreover, there were another dozen seminars all across the nation. Her New Age books have sold over seven million copies world wide, leading the way for hundreds of other New Age book titles, which, taken together, now outnumber traditional religious books in virtually every American bookstore.

I already knew that what Shirley MacLaine was preaching was rank heresy, but I was not prepared for what happened at the seminar. There was talk of 'centring', 'cosmic energy', 'chakras', healing crystals, and 'consciousness raising'. There were attempted demonstrations of aura sensing. But the shocker of the day came suddenly out of nowhere.

Having encouraged us to take responsibility for our own lives, Ms MacLaine turned directly to us and said matter-of-factly: 'As Jesus and Buddha have said, "Be still and know that *you* are God."' The audience drank it in as a great revealed truth, unaware that neither Buddha nor Jesus had ever said that.

It seemed not to matter to either Ms MacLaine or her audience that it was the great lie of the ages, dating all the way back to the Garden of Eden when Satan said to Eve, you will be like God (Gen. 3:5). If some of the lies being told by the New Age Movement are subtle variations from the truth, this supreme lie is by no means subtle. It is a 180-degree twisting of the truth. In fact, it is a blasphemous reversal of Scripture which puts us in the place of God. 'Be still, and know that *I* am God;' from Psalm 46:10, refers to the God of Creation, not to us. From the mouth of God, its message is plain and simple: God is God and, make no mistake about it, we are not.

Deception in a Garden

Yet perhaps there was some confusion about what Shirley MacLaine was saying. Did she really intend to say that *we* are God? Certainly, my friend at the fundraising event would not have said it so strongly. 'Part of the oneness of God', perhaps, or 'filled with the divine spark', but not 'I am God'. It wasn't long before Ms MacLaine put us through an exercise intended to lead each of us to our 'Higher Self'. That was, after all, the purpose of the seminar – to get in touch with higher self. But who *was*, or what *is*, higher self?

The lights in the ballroom were lowered, and meditative windchime music played on cue in the background. Closing our eyes as instructed, we listened while Ms MacLaine talked us through a visualisation sequence which took us into a lofty flight of fancy above the earth, then down into a cool, wet garden, then across a bridge to a large opening. 'There before you', she fairly whispered, 'is a large tree, larger than any of the other trees. Standing before you beneath the tree is the one you have come to seek. Let me introduce you to your Higher Self. Your higher self is the one to whom you have been praying. Your higher self is God!'

The quietness of the room was penetrated by first one person, then another, softly crying. For many people, it obviously was a very moving experience. I opened my eyes and looked around with amazement, wondering how eight hundred people could be led so easily to the belief that the God to whom they had offered a lifetime of prayers was actually themselves.

It did not escape my attention that the great lie had been presented to the audience in the context of a garden, and that the focal point of the lie was associated with a tree. Nothing has changed since the great lie was first told in the Garden of Eden regarding the forbidden fruit of the tree. Because a garden and a tree were successful the first time round, Satan must think he can use the same props over and over again with guaranteed success.

I Am God; I Am God!

There was no longer any doubt about what Shirley had meant earlier in saying, 'Be still and know that *you* are God.' It was the culmination of her own experience when, with claimed reluctance, she first came to that realisation herself. In *Out On a Limb*, Shirley was told by her friend and spiritual mentor, David, that she was God. In her American television adaptation of that book, the scene is dramatised on the beach in Malibu near Shirley's home.

David tells Shirley that all the answers about life are within her, because she is God. When Shirley wonders aloud whether she might not become arrogant if she really believed she were God, David's response is one of reassurance. 'Say to yourself that you are God,' he tells Shirley. With only slight hesitation, she says quietly, 'I am God.' 'No, louder,' says David. 'Say it louder.' Once again, but louder, Shirley says, 'I am God.' Her words are still not said with sufficient conviction for David, so one last time he says, 'Turn to the ocean and say it like you really mean it!' Obediently, Shirley turns to the ocean, stretches out her arms, and with full conviction shouts out, 'I AM GOD!'

The camera holds tight on that scene, then fades away into a commercial break. It was a dramatic moment. It was *the* moment, because it was the central message of the book and of the film. It is also the central message of the New Age Movement: I am God; you are God.

Redefining God

How can one possibly believe that he or she is God? It is happening with such frequency today that there must be *some* reason. It happens, first of all, through a redefinition of God. The traditional, Biblical definition of a Creator God of the universe would not permit any of us to claim his status. We know that we did not create the universe in which we live. Indeed, *could* not! So the New Age world view supplies us with a radically-different scenario of God and Creation.

In the New Age, God is no longer the personal God of the Bible, who interacts with Man and works his will through history. Rather, God is an impersonal God *force*, of which everything in the universe is a part. It is much the same as *Star Wars*' catch-phrase, 'May the Force be with you.'

In the New Age, as in much of Eastern mysticism and Greek philosophy, all is said to be *one* – whether matter, energy, or consciousness. The appropriate label is *monism*. Therefore, the resulting equation follows: all is one; God is one; we are one; therefore we are God. It's neat, it's clean, and sufficiently convincing for anyone who wants to believe it.

The New Age version of creation is somewhat more bizarre. In the beginning, so it is said, the God force was a sleeping, slumbering, pulsating ball of energy. When it roused itself, it exploded, in Big Bang fashion, into billions and billions of individualised points of consciousness – each one of which became a soul. These souls – all of which were God – found their way into the three-dimensional earth-plane and soon began to think of themselves as three-dimensional as well. (No clear explanation is given as to how the three-dimensional earth-plane itself came into existence.) When they began to think and act three-dimensionally, they forgot that they were God. Their higher selves became only lower selves – humans, with finite human thoughts.

The goal of the New Age, therefore, is to raise our consciousness into realising that who we really are is God. That we have been God from the very beginning and can be God once again if only we acknowledge the illusion of our earthly existence. By admitting our godhood, we are able to transcend time and space and reconnect with the God that we are: infinite, cosmic, omnipotent.

Conceding that we can never achieve such a leap of logic, or even of faith, in one lifetime, our spiritual evolution is made possible through hundreds, if not thousands, of lifetimes. It is here that New Age thinking merges with yet another lie, the idea of reincarnation. Reincarnation becomes the change agent through which the soul is brought to the ultimate realisation of its godhood.

The important point here is that, by New Age thinking, there is no separation between each of us and God. God is not outside of ourselves. We are all part of a God force which has lost its way. However, what does that leave us with? A God who could forget who he is? What kind of a God could that possibly be? Is this weak God a God that we should want even *ourselves* to be? If it is enlightenment we seek, how can we turn to an entity that doesn't know who he, or it, really is?

Shirley MacLaine and other New Age proponents are not getting us in touch with higher self. Instead, they are degrading our lower selves to undifferentiated humanity lost in deception. They are dragging down any notion of divinity to the lowest common denominator, wherein God is not different from ourselves, or evil, or pollution, or a grubworm! If all truly is one, then neither God nor Man is greater than animals, plants, or the minutest of subatomic particles.

Is is not enough that we should have been created 'in the image of God' (Gen. 1:27)? Have we not enough honour to have been singled out from among all creation as rulers over the earth (Gen. 1:28)? Must we fall once again from the precipice of pride, only to discover that we fell victim to the great lie? It was the Creator of our universe who said, 'Be still and know that I am God.' Wishing it otherwise won't make it so. Given our need for strength to cope with circumstances over which we are powerless, who would even *want* to wish it so?

Reason To Shudder

My travels to speak out against the New Age Movement took me on one occasion to San Francisco for a Donahue-type TV chat show. The studio audience was mesmerised; I was greatly horrified. J.Z. Knight was the star of the show, telling us how the 35,000-year-old entity known as Ramtha had mysteriously come into her life, how he had begun using her as a channel through which to bring his cosmic insight to the many thousands of New Age converts who have now attended Knight's seminars. Charming, witty and humorous, this extremely attractive New Age heroine was the epitome of femininity – nothing like the strong male personality she assumes when supposedly possessed by Ramtha.

When 'clips' of her channelling sessions were shown to the studio and television audience, J.Z. watched the monitor with a reserved smile. I wondered if she saw herself with great curiosity, fascinated with what she looks like when her 'soul has left her body', as she claims; or whether perhaps she was amused that so many people took her act seriously. (A former associate quit in disgust after allegedly overhearing Ms Knight practising her Ramtha voice in a pre-channelling-session warm-up.)

Even if it was all a sham, I was far more disturbed by Knight's book *Ramtha* (Sovereign Press, 1986), than

Shirley MacLaine's *Out On a Limb*. Where MacLaine's book is fanciful and outrageous, Knight's book is nothing but scary. It is frightening enough to read Marilyn Ferguson's New Age handbook, *The Aquarian Conspiracy*, in which she *describes* what I believe to be the work of Satan through the New Age Movement. Yet the chilling feeling I had while reading *Ramtha*, was that it *was* the work of Satan! *Ramtha* is such a blatant exchange of truth for error that I kept saying to myself, 'No human alone wrote this. This book literally could be from the pen of Satan himself.'

Whatever its origin, *Ramtha* presents the purest, least disguised doctrine of the New Age Movement that I have read. Perhaps this partially accounts for its shocking nature. It also is the least ashamed presentation of the moral chaos fostered by its doctrine, embarrassing as that ought to be. No other book of which I am aware presents so clearly the New Age beliefs that we are God, that we each have our own truth, that we create our own reality, that we choose everything that happens to us, that there is neither good nor evil, that no one has a right to judge our actions, and that we are accountable only to ourselves.

A Case of Unabashed Blasphemy

Nor is any book I have ever read so openly blasphemous as *Ramtha*. Just a few excerpts will give you a taste of what I mean:

> Yeshua ben Joseph, whom you call Jesus of Nazareth, is a great god, just as you are a great god. But he is not the only son of God; he is *a* son of God. He was a man who *became* God, just as you will become God (p. 36).

> Yeshua is your brother, not your saviour (p. 37).
>
> A Christ is anyone who realises that he is God and *lives* that truth (p. 36).
>
> Love the beautiful entity that you are and the God that you are – and cease reading your insidious Book [the Bible]! (p. 38).
>
> In your BOOK OF BOOKS [the Bible, John 1:1] it says: 'In the beginning was the Word, and all was with the Word.' Most improper! The Word was *nothing* without the Thought, for thought is the basis and creator of everything that is (p. 79).
>
> Everything your religions have taught you could be wrong. Do you know what is wonderful about that? It means that perhaps there really is no such thing as a devil, or hell, or sin, or damnation, or a fearsome God – that they could be wrong. And they *are* (p. 90).

I hasten to remind you that this teaching comes from one of the most widely acclaimed spokespersons in the New Age Movement in America. If J. Z. Knight is unfamiliar to the British public, many more familiar Britons are beginning to espouse her message. Nor is her teaching out of line in the least with what is being taught by others in the Movement: God is not God, we are. Jesus was not the one and only Son of God, and he was not the exclusive Messiah and Christ of prophecy. We too can be Christ. What's more, the Bible is deceiving us about every essential doctrine it proclaims.

Near the end of the programme on which J.Z. Knight and I were guests, the host of the show asked me what was so wrong with people believing in Ramtha. I got the impression that he felt it was all very faddish, mere fun and games. Certainly, it was good entertainment for his own programme. However, my heartfelt response was much more serious than he expected. Referring with a heavy burden to the *Ramtha* book itself, I told him that we were dealing with nothing short of blasphemy.

When I mentioned the word *blasphemy*, a distinct hush came over the audience, and the host did an obvious mental doubletake. It was only at that point in the programme that my message got a fair hearing. For all their fascination with channellers, psychics and the New Age Movement, praise God that among the religiously confused people of America there is still a residual sense of respect for the God of Creation and for his revealed Scriptures.

Where that sense of awe and respect is casually tossed out the window, we are headed for certain trouble. You can see it easily in J.Z. Knight's book. There is a predictable progression from the dethronement of God, to the divinity of Man, to the abandonment of an eternal judgment, to the exaltation of personal choice, to the denial of good and evil, to the demise of morality.

That is why the eventual appearance of the New Age Movement in Britain is so potentially lethal. It will capitalise on the existing environment of relative morality and secular humanism, and make the not-so-quantum leap to a broadly-accepted religion of avowed blasphemy wherein self-rule takes on a cosmic justification.

Blasphemy With The Slightest Shift

Fortunately, we still have some time before there are large groups of people running around Britain, as presently in America, proudly proclaiming, 'I am God.' Even so, I already see significant groundwork being laid by some who speak on behalf of Christianity in this country. Take, for example, this little devotional item appearing near the time of Lent in one of the major newspapers last year. The seemingly-innocent meditation took on an ever-so-subtle shift away from Scripture:

> Jesus must at some time later have confided in his first disciples the inner experience of his baptism in the Jordan near Jericho. In that experience he had heard an *inner voice* assuring him that he was loved and approved by God, and had felt an infusion of spiritual power as clearly *as if* a dove from Heaven had lighted upon him [emphasis mine].

I am certain that we shall never know exactly what transpired on the occasion of Jesus's baptism. The event is truly one of those 'divine mysteries' of which the Bishop of Durham is so fond. Yet a straightforward reading of the Scripture suggests that the writer's characterisation of the event's being only internal may be far from the mark:

> When all the people were being baptised, Jesus was baptised too. And as he was praying, heaven was opened and the Holy Spirit descended on him in *bodily form* like a dove. And a voice came from heaven: 'You are my Son, whom I love; with you I am well pleased' (Luke 3:21–2).

Nor did John the Baptist put such an exclusively mystical gloss on the appearance of the Spirit to Jesus:

> Then John gave this testimony: 'I saw the Spirit come down from heaven as a dove and remain on him. I would not have known him, except that the one who sent me to baptise with water told me, "The man on whom you see the Spirit come down and remain is he who will baptise with the Holy Spirit"' (John 1:32–3).

Whatever else the appearance of the Holy Spirit meant, it clearly was more than a private inner experience that Jesus felt unobservable by anyone else. John *saw* whatever manifestation it was, and had been told in advance by God that it would be a sign of the Messiah.

Alarm bells begin to sound when someone implies that Jesus discovered an inner spark of divinity (which all of us share), or listened to a unique call of God (as if he were not himself God). Or, more especially, when Jesus is made merely symbolic of a mystical experience in which we all share. Writing from his 'Pulpit' (*Sunday Times*, March 26th, 1989), Gerald Priestland gives us a good example of a failure to distinguish between the Christ of Jesus and the 'Christ within all of us'.

Priestland expressed gratitude that the Shroud of Turin failed to provide modern scientific evidence of Jesus's resurrection. 'The resurrection would then have become a unique compulsory fact instead of a perpetual myth of how the God in human kind suffers only to rise again.' What is important for Priestland is that Christ personifies each of us, 'For Christ had become everyman – and everywoman, I dare say. No longer need we be distracted by his particularity, for He has become like any of us, and in that form at last He spreads through the world.'

I wish I could give Priestland the benefit of the doubt and join with him in the wonderful *analogy* that indeed we are Jesus's hands today, doing what Jesus would do; and his feet, going where he would go. Unfortunately, that is not the crucial end of the message when God incarnate is made to be mystical:

> There is no God Up There, a yawning gap, and Us Down Here, but a continuous circulation of love received and returned. Clogged and faulty the exchange may be but it is renewed by every Easter. For it is not a matter of who Jesus was, but who He is.

Call me suspicious, but I can't help but think that this minimalistic view of Jesus is a dangerous step towards declaring our own divinity. Priestland is right, of course. There is no yawning gap between us and God. The gap has been filled by Jesus Christ, who, though he became fully human, never ceased to be fully divine – and divine in a way which we shall never be. He was and is divine *by nature*, whereas we are *adopted* into the family of the one God – Father, Son and Holy Spirit. It is this, quite different, doctrinal picture of Christ which Paul paints in his letter to the Colossians:

> He is the image of the invisible God, the firstborn over all creation. For by him all things were created: things in heaven and on earth, visible and invisible, whether thrones or powers or rulers or authorities; all things were created by him and for him. He is before all things, and in him all things hold together. And he is the head of the body, the church; he is the beginning and the firstborn from among the dead, so that in everything he might have the supremacy. For God was pleased to have all his fullness dwell in him, and through him to reconcile to himself all things, whether things on earth or things in heaven, by making peace through his blood, shed on the cross (Col. 1:15–20).

That sounds like a fairly *particularised* Christ to me! I'm afraid that Priestland's view of Jesus takes us into dangerous territory.

It is very nearly the same dangerous territory into which we were taken by Kazantzakis and Scorsese in *The Last Temptation of Christ*. In their minds, Jesus did not die for the redemption of our sins. He merely demonstrated through his life how we can actually save ourselves! By their view, we each have our own crosses to bear, but if – like Jesus – we overcome, then we too are Christ. Like

Jesus, we become divine. Like Shirley MacLaine and J.Z. Knight, we become *God*! Given its blasphemous message, the movie was mistitled. More appropriate would have been, *The First and Greatest Temptation of Man*.

It's time we stopped playing around with the sacrilege of reducing Christ to the level of our own humanity. The next door we open will lead to the blasphemy of our own godhood. Unfortunately, the coming of the New Age Movement will be all the incentive many will need to cross that threshold.

13

The Language of Blasphemy

Blasphemy In Everyday Speech

> And each blasphemer quite escape the rod,
> Because the insult's not on man but God?
> > Pope
> > *Epilogue to Satires*

At an early age, I cultivated a verbal sharpness which ranged from harmless teasing to not-so-harmless sarcasm. (I should have guessed even then that I should end up being a lawyer!) Perhaps aware of my potential for misusing words, my parents were strict about the language coming out of my mouth. I can recall at least one occasion where unacceptable words caused my mouth to be washed out. The revolting taste of soap lingers in my memory even now!

By this time you must be imagining terribly vile language spewing from the lips of a brash young boy testing his parents' patience – probably a series of four-letter words fit for the walls of a public toilet. I must confess that some of them *were* four-letter words – like 'gosh' and 'darn'. There were also five- and three-letter

The Language of Blasphemy

words, such as 'golly' and 'gee'. Surprised? I must say that it was not easy for me, either, as a youngster of ten to appreciate the wickedness of language which seemed benignly common to the schoolyard.

Looking back now, I realise that the explanation given for such forbidden words was my first introduction to the notion of blasphemy. 'Gosh' and 'golly' were lighter terms for *God*, I was told. 'Gee' was a short form of *Jesus*. And 'darn' was awfully darn close to 'damn'. It always intrigued me that it was okay, however, to say 'goodness me' or 'goodness gracious', if one so chose. Likewise, news of tragedy invariably was accompanied by an unembarrassed 'Oh, my goodness!' But then, I suppose consistency was never a great virtue.

Impertinent as I was, I also questioned why 'damn' and 'hell' – words I never actually used – were off limits. Nothing I had seen in the Bible seemed to outlaw their use. In fact, the Bible itself was *filled* with 'damns' and 'hells'. However, it did not escape my attention that the Bible was also filled with references to God, and, before long, the point of it all slowly began to sink into my young mind. Good church-going folk that I knew didn't use serious Biblical terms loosely just to spice up their conversation. Spiritually significant words were reserved for spiritually significant conversations. I could always tell which crowd I was with by the language they chose to use.

Call it societal brainwashing, if you will, or spiritual complacency, perhaps, but I no longer take the slightest passing notice of another's 'golly', 'gosh', or 'gee'. I admit, too, that my conscience has been numbed as well by the constant barrage of 'damns' and 'hells' which fill the workplace and spill nightly into our homes via television. I still don't use any of those terms myself – well, perhaps an occasional 'gee'. Even hitting my thumb with a hammer is likely to evoke only a rather silly expletive substitute, like 'cottonpick it!' (I know. It hardly justifies the effort to get it out of my mouth!)

On the other hand, I am still startled when Christians, especially, lace their talk with casual references to God. 'Oh my God' may be a more honest version of 'Oh, my goodness' in the face of real tragedy. Yet that is not the way I most often hear it used. Typically, it is just an offhanded phrase used as part of any garden-variety excited utterance. Curiously, from many of my Christian friends I often hear a subtle, mid-word change in inflection. What would have been 'Oh, my God' ends up being 'Oh, my go-sh,' softening the expression just that little bit. I always wonder which word would have completed the phrase had the person been in a different setting.

Looking Beyond the Words

Lest you think that a book on so serious a subject as blasphemy has quickly deteriorated into petty word distinctions for the pious, let me hasten to make the point of it all. Blasphemy originated with words in mind. Words about God. Words which display a casual regard for God. Or worse yet, words which betray a contemptuous *disregard* for God.

God himself uses words very carefully, as if words can have a profound spiritual effect on us ('Man does not live on bread alone, but on every word that comes from the mouth of God.'). Not to be outdone, Satan also loves a clever turn of phrase ('You shall *not* surely die'). However, God claims unique possession of the term 'word' itself. Appropriately, his divine revelation, recorded for us in writing, is called the Word ('Blessed are those who hear the word of God and obey it.'). And, as we have seen, in his own incarnation as Jesus the Messiah, he is depicted *personally* as the Word ('In the beginning was the Word, and the Word was with God, and the Word was God.').

It should not be surprising, then, that God should call us into strict account for the way in which we ourselves use words, nor that the psalmist should pray, 'May the words of my mouth and the meditation of my heart be pleasing in your sight, O Lord, my Rock and my Redeemer' (Ps. 19:14). As the psalmist intimates, there is a connection between the words of our mouths and the thoughts of our hearts. Our words reveal our inner thoughts and feelings, our attitudes and values. Jesus said, 'But the things that come out of the mouth come from the heart, and these make a man "unclean"' (Matt. 15:18).

Showing Contempt for God

If my parents' concern about 'golly', 'gosh', and 'gee' bordered on the hypertechnical, it also proceeded from a legitimate scriptural source. Reverence for God was commanded in the words, 'Do not blaspheme God or curse the ruler of your people' (Exod. 22:28). And also, 'You shall not misuse the name of the Lord your God, for the Lord will not hold anyone guiltless who misuses his name' (Deut. 5:11). Rabbinical Jews took this commandment so literally that they would avoid even *saying* the name of God, if possible, lest they misuse it.

By Jewish tradition, it is said that Moses would not mention the name of the Holy One (Blessed be He) until after he had spoken twenty-one words. Moses took his cue, so Jewish scholars taught, from the ministering angels, who spoke the name of God only following the threefold sanctification found in Isaiah 6:3, 'And they were calling to one another: "Holy, holy, holy, is the Lord Almighty"'. Said Moses, according to this tradition, 'It is enough for me to be seven times as modest as the ministering angels.' And therefore the lesson for the pious Jew was that, if someone so great as Moses would mention God's name only after twenty-one words, how much more must one be careful not to take God's name in vain. (See *Sifre*, A Tannaitic Commentary on Deuteronomy, *Piska* 306.)

Remarkable procedures were invented to ensure that no blasphemy was perpetuated. First of all, none of the Old Testament references to blasphemy actually cites the forbidden words, for fear thereby of committing the crime. Second, when it came to prosecuting a person for blasphemy, a special procedure was devised relating to the evidence against the accused. During the trial itself, the witness was required to substitute other words for the alleged blasphemy, the actual words being silently understood by the judges. Yet because the court could not convict the accused of the offence without hearing the exact words used, the court was cleared at the time of sentencing and the witness was then asked to repeat the blasphemous words. Upon hearing the blasphemy, the judges would tear their robes as a sign of grief, and then proceed to pass the sentence. Rather obviously, we have come a long way from such displays of moral outrage in today's morally-lax society, in which the tearing of one's clothes is likely to be nothing more than a fashion trend among young people.

Sidestepping the Serious

The seriousness of Jewish blasphemy was seen in the penalty which attached, being death. In one case, God had commanded the death of a young man of mixed race who had reviled the name of God in an altercation with an Israelite.

> Now the son of an Israelite mother and an Egyptian father went out among the Israelites, and a fight broke out in the camp between him and an Israelite. The son of the Israelite woman blasphemed the Name with a curse; so they brought him to Moses. (His mother's name was Shelomith, the daughter of Dibri the Danite.) They put him in custody until the will of the Lord should be made clear to them. Then the LORD said to Moses: 'Take the blasphemer outside the camp. All those who heard him are to lay their hands on his head, and the entire assembly is to stone him' (Lev. 24:10–14).

Yet as is so often the case with seemingly harsh laws, exceptions were carved out by the Jews in order to narrow the impact of blasphemy convictions. According to the Talmud, only a cursing of the *name* of the Lord (YHVH) merited the death penalty. Other lesser blasphemies (for example, reviling the name *Adonai* or *Elohim*) more likely incurred the penalty of excommunication. In fact, there was some authority insisting that, in order to merit the death penalty, a curse against God actually had to invoke God's name as part of the curse (for example, 'In the name of YHVH may YHVH be cursed')!

Unlike other religions, Judaism did not extend blasphemy to the reviling of sacred institutions, customs, or people. Speaking disrespectfully to God, or doubting his power, or even comparing God to idols surely was as contemptuous in its effect, if not more so, as was a curse against God. However, in such instances no blasphemy prosecution would be brought. With Jesus, of course, the Jewish leaders managed to find a strong case for blasphemy in his claim to be the one and only Son of God. (If they had been right *factually* – if he was not the Son of God – they would have been right in their conclusion. Such a claim, unsupported by demonstrations of divine power, would have been the ultimate blasphemy.)

In the larger picture, the Jews' ever-narrowing interpretation of blasphemy may indicate the extent to which the empty legalism of institutionalised Judaism had robbed the Jews of a vibrant, passionate faith in God. It also stands as a warning to us that any concern regarding the nature and extent of specific blasphemy laws must remain secondary to the far more compelling question of how seriously we take our own faith. Have we been more outraged by a single verbal assault on God's name than by the daily, ongoing threat to faith by those, even within the Church, who vilify the Scriptures and empty the Gospel of its power?

On the Page, Or In the Heart?

Like good lawyers, most of us invariably look for any loopholes we might be able to find in God's laws; and, like little children, too often we try to get as close as possible to doing what we know we shouldn't. Can you remember when profanities referring to the Deity in novels and other books were thought to be all right as long as they were abbreviated so as not to spell out the entire name? We were given, for example, only a representative 'G-d d-mn'. Can it be that God is any less offended when profanities of his name are presented in literature with some of the letters missing? Of course, modern literature prides itself in filling in all the blanks for us, whether linguistic or even sexual. Nevertheless, there used to be at least a formalised respect for the names of God and Christ. Society demanded it, expected it, and was shocked if it didn't get it. No longer.

At this point, I must confess to a change in the literary form by which I myself refer to God. Owing to accepted custom, in my earliest writings I invariably capitalised the pronouns of deity (for example, 'Jesus told *His* disciples . . .'). Now, however, consistent with the less-formalised modern translations of the Bible, I use the accepted style which puts pronouns of the deity in lower case ('Jesus told *his* disciples . . .'). However far I may miss the mark, I attempt to make my writing 'user-friendly' for contemporary readers. For many of them, outdated, High Church literary form could stand in the way. Yet a more traditional publisher recently reversed my decision and restored capitalised pronouns to my manuscript.

I can't say if God cares whether pronouns referring to him are capitalised, but I can say with confidence that he cares whether we have capitalised *him* in our lives.

Single Words Make Whole Statements

This brings us back to the Third Commandment: 'You shall not misuse the name of the Lord your God, for the Lord will not hold anyone guiltless who misuses his name' (Exod. 20:7). Is this commandment limited in scope to blaspheming the name of God, taking it in vain, or using it profanely? Is swearing in God's name the only object of this divine injunction?

The person who swears, saying 'By God . . . this' or 'By God . . . that' is most certainly using God's name in vain, and thereby *misusing* the name of our heavenly Father. Likewise, the use of 'Jesus Christ' as a common expletive (as in 'Jeesus!' or 'Jeesus Christ!'), is both profane and blasphemous. Yet in each case, undoubtedly, something more is going on behind the scenes. Have you ever stopped to consider what might have occasioned the first use of the name 'Jesus Christ' as profanity? Who was the first person to use it that way? Why would he have chosen to make disrespectful use of a name which previously had only been used with the greatest of respect?

My guess is that his intention was to deny the affirmation inherent within the name-and-title combination, 'Jesus Christ' – that is, to express angry disbelief at the very thought that Jesus of Nazareth was indeed the Messiah of God. 'Jesus, the Messiah? Not a chance!' is the idea. It would be as if someone were to tell us that Margaret Thatcher had defected to the Communists. 'Thatcher a Communist!' we might respond with disbelieving denial.

'Jeesus Christ' is not just an expletive which ought to be deleted from our vocabularies. It is a statement about what we believe. It is a reflection of how we regard our Saviour. No conscientious Christian could let the name above all names pass his lips without the reverence which it is due. A profane use of Jesus's name would be inconsistent with one's professed faith in Jesus as Lord. It is bad enough for the unbeliever that such profanity would be blasphemy, but, for a Christian, such blasphemy borders on apostasy.

I realise that unbelievers throw around Jesus's name loosely without any conscious intent to make a theological judgment about Jesus one way or the other. I doubt if many, if any, have ever stopped to think of what they are implying in the misuse of his name. Even so, I am fascinated that the name of Jesus has become so common a swearword, particularly in a 'Christian society'. In a pluralistic society, which is what we really have, why isn't *Buddha's* name equally defiled? (Do we sense intuitively that Buddha is not really a force to be reckoned with?) And why not Muhammad? (Are we reminded again that others may take their religion more seriously than we do?)

Certainly, at a minimum, the almost exclusive abuse of Jesus's name mirrors an *unbelieving* 'Christian society'. (In the workplace, his name is heard more on the lips of *unbelievers* than *believers*!) But more than that, it may be Satan's way of cheapening regard for the person of Christ. To win the battle for faith, Satan doesn't have to get us to curse God with invective – rather, just to take God for granted. Just to ignore his majesty and sovereignty. Why should we submit to the lordship of someone whose name we toss about with the same banality as vulgar references to cow manure?

14

Jesus the Blasphemer

The Ultimate Irony – Man Accusing God

> And I say, there was never man thus abused . . .
> William Shakespeare
> *Twelfth Night*

Why do people often call others derisive names which more appropriately apply to themselves? Is it because they know intuitively what they are, and try to pre-empt others from being the first to say it? Is it a classic defence mechanism? Whatever the reason, one of the sad ironies recorded by Scripture is the allegation by any number of people that Jesus himself – God in human flesh – was a blasphemer.

In Jesus's case, of course, even a sincere person legitimately might have accused Jesus of blasphemy, because he not only *claimed* to be God, but he also *acted* as if he were God. Had he been wrong about that, then blasphemy would have been the right charge to bring against him. But, oh, how dramatically he acquitted himself! Take, for example, the case of Jesus's healing of the paralytic:

> Some men brought to him a paralytic, lying on a mat. When Jesus saw their faith, he said to the paralytic, 'Take heart, son; your sins are forgiven.'
> At this, some of the teachers of the law said to themselves, 'This fellow is blaspheming!'
> Knowing their thoughts, Jesus said, 'Why do you entertain evil thoughts in your hearts? Which is easier: to say, "Your sins are forgiven," or to say, "Get up and walk"? But so that you may know that the Son of Man has authority on earth to forgive sins. . . .' Then he said to the paralytic, 'Get up, take your mat and go home.' And the man got up and went home. When the crowd saw this, they were filled with awe; and they praised God, who had given such authority to men (Matt. 9:2–8).

If we are honest with ourselves, we probably would have joined those who accused Jesus of blasphemy. What could be more presumptuous than claiming the ability to forgive sins? Everyone knows that forgiving sins is God's prerogative. True, some aren't too sure about sin itself, and perhaps there are many people who are sceptical about the whole idea of forgiveness and salvation. Yet if there *is* sin, and if there *is* such a thing as salvation, then we all know whose right it would be to forgive sin. God's and God's alone.

So into the picture walks Jesus, boldly declaring that a man's sins are forgiven. Is it any wonder that the religious establishment would accuse him of blasphemy?

I love this passage! Jesus could have performed miracles all day long, as he did in the healing of this paralytic, and there still would be doubts about who he was. Some might claim trickery or psychosomatic self-healing, and never attribute the healing to Jesus *as God*. However,

Jesus puts the issue squarely on the line, saying: 'Your sins are forgiven.' Then, when the crowd reacts with hostile accusations of blasphemy, Jesus demonstrates his divine right to forgive by demonstrating his divine power to heal. It was the ultimate fact of his divinity that he was demonstrating. His *unique divinity* was the crucial point!

When New Agers say that they themselves have within them the 'spark of divinity', they are not talking about being 'created in the image of God' with all the grandeur that implies. No, they are claiming to be a part of the 'oneness of God', which, not too loosely translated, means that they *are* God. However, in one divine statement backed up by one divine act, Jesus puts an end to such nonsense. Can we heal a paralytic upon our *own* command? Can we, with any reasonable basis for doing so, forgive a person's sins against God? How quickly blasphemy is turned on its ear! It was not the one and only Son of God who blasphemed. It is we who blaspheme when we reject the person of Jesus, who was God among us.

I must admit that I tire of hearing that Jesus never claimed to be the unique Son of God. From New Agers to Jehovah's Witnesses to headline-stealing liberal theologians, the cry is that Jesus was merely *a* son of God, merely one of *many* sons of God. That we, too, can be a son of God in the exact same sense. After all, comes the challenge, did not Jesus say, 'You are all gods' (John 10:34)? It hardly matters that Jesus was referring to Psalm 82:6, where the judges of Israel are depicted as 'gods' in dispensing God's justice on earth, nor that the very next line says, 'But you will die like mere men, you will fall like every other ruler.' Everyone lately seems to be rewriting the story of Jesus with a humanistic pen.

But Jesus's claim to being a fully-human, fully-God incarnation of the Creator – mysterious as that is to us – was certainly not lost on the very people who saw him

Jesus the Blasphemer

and heard him while he was on this earth. Look closely at this exchange:

> 'I and the Father are one.' Again the Jews picked up stones to stone him, but Jesus said to them, 'I have shown you many great miracles from the Father. For which of these do you stone me?' 'We are not stoning you for any of these,' replied the Jews, 'but for blasphemy, because you, a mere man, claim to be God' (John 10:30–3).

Note once again that it is not the miracles themselves for which the religious establishment wanted to kill Jesus. It was for his claim to be God! Not just *a* god among many, but *the* God. The *one* God!

Another exchange between Jesus and a group of sceptical Jews really puts the issue in sharp focus. It occurs when Jesus is so bold as to say that anyone who keeps his word will not die. The Jews then ask him point-blank, 'Are you greater than our father Abraham? He died, and so did the prophets. Who do you think you are?' (John 8:53). His answer ought to grab the attention of both sceptics (who deny Jesus's claims to being God) and Muslims (who place great stock in their lineage from Abraham):

> 'I tell you the truth,' Jesus answered, 'before Abraham was born, I am!' At this, they picked up stones to stone him . . . (John 8:58–9).

Jesus claimed to be 'I am' – the Eternal One, the Preexistent One, the Creator, the One God!

Any doubt of this issue is resolved in a review of the formal charges brought against Jesus before the illegally-convened Sanhedrin. Try to imagine the scene – the chief priests huddled together, eagerly looking for some tiny bit of evidence with which to condemn him, and Jesus finally looking up, shocking them with stronger evidence against himself than they could ever have hoped for:

> The chief priests and the whole Sanhedrin were looking for false evidence against Jesus so that they could put him to death. But they did not find any, though many false witnesses came forward.
>
> Finally two came forward and declared, 'This fellow said, "I am able to destroy the temple of God and rebuild it in three days."'
>
> Then the high priest stood up and said to Jesus, 'Are you not going to answer? What is this testimony that these men are bringing against you?' But Jesus remained silent.
>
> The high priest said to him, 'I charge you under oath by the living God: Tell us if you are the Christ, the Son of God.'
>
> 'Yes, it is as you say,' Jesus replied. 'But I say to all of you: In the future you will see the Son of Man sitting at the right hand of the Mighty One and coming on the clouds of heaven.'
>
> Then the high priest tore his clothes and said, 'He has spoken blasphemy! Why do we need any more witnesses? Look, now you have heard the blasphemy. What do you think?'
>
> 'He is worthy of death,' they answered (Matt. 26:59–66).

We are not talking here about a Rushdie-type death threat for having *offended* a prophet of God (whoever one might understand God's chosen prophet to be). We are talking about nothing short of claiming to *be* the prophet. Even more, it was nothing short of claiming to be co-equal with 'the Mighty One' – that is, to *be God*! (It's as if Rushdie had claimed to be Allah.)

As a lawyer, I revel in the drama of this courtroom

scene. Here the prosecutor asks Jesus to testify under oath *by the living God* as to who he is. In actuality what Jesus says is, 'I am the very living God by whom you have just asked me to swear!' Can't you just see the expression on the prosecutor's face? Is it any wonder that they hurriedly put our Saviour to death?

Frankly, but for the blinding self-righteousness which led them to miss the Messiah, I could wish that we had the same sense of outrage against those today who, far from being God, claim equal status with Jesus. Yet what divine irony that the Son of God should be charged, convicted and put to death for the crime of blasphemy. Truly he *did* bear our own sins of blasphemy on the cross!

The Unforgivable Sin

The remarkable thing about these false accusations of Jesus (sincerely brought as they might have been on the part of some, and spitefully on the part of others) is that Jesus never took the offence personally. He was not bothered by the fact that – as a person – he was falsely accused, humiliated and reviled. To the very end ('Father, forgive them, for they do not know what they are doing.'), Jesus's interest was in the souls of his accusers. Understanding both Jesus's nature and character helps us to appreciate more fully the so-called 'unforgivable sin'. Although Jesus spoke of it in the context of blasphemy, we almost never hear it referred to with that context in mind.

It would be hard to say how many people have wallowed in a lifetime of self-condemnation and agonising guilt, believing that *theirs* is the unforgivable sin, whatever the sin may be. There just seems to be a feeling in a lot of people that the sins of everyone but themselves can be forgiven. Perhaps it stems from the fact that we each know ourselves – both good and bad – in a way that no one else does. Just as we often tend to think that our 'good' is better than others' 'good', we too often tend to assume that our 'bad' is worse than others' 'bad'. Sometimes *unforgivably* bad!

Tragically, there has been more than one person whose overwhelming feelings of guilt have led to what many others believe to be the 'unforgivable sin': suicide. Because a person who commits suicide deprives himself of an opportunity to repent, suicide has taken on what may be a wholly undeserved reputation. It's not, of course, that suicide is a morally acceptable 'way out'. It's just that Jesus never directly addressed the issue of suicide, and clearly did not have it in mind when he taught about a kind of sin which is without forgiveness.

If, then, those two applications miss the point, what are we to make of the 'unforgivable sin', particularly as it applies to blasphemy? Let's take a closer look at the passage in its proper context:

> Then they brought him a demon-possessed man who was blind and mute, and Jesus healed him, so that he could both talk and see. All the people were astonished and said, 'Could this be the Son of David?'
>
> But when the Pharisees heard this, they said, 'It is only by Beelzebub, the prince of demons, that this fellow drives out demons.'
>
> Jesus knew their thoughts and said to them, 'Every kingdom divided against itself will be ruined, and every city or household divided against itself will not stand. If Satan drives out Satan, he is divided against himself. How then can his kingdom stand? And if I drive out demons by Beelzebub, by whom do your people drive them out? So then, they will be your judges. But if I drive out demons by the Spirit of God, then the kingdom of God has come upon you.
>
> 'He who is not with me is against me, and he who does not gather with me scatters. And so I tell you,

Jesus the Blasphemer

every sin and blasphemy will be forgiven men, but the blasphemy against the Spirit will not be forgiven. Anyone who speaks a word against the Son of Man will be forgiven, but anyone who speaks against the Holy Spirit will not be forgiven, either in this age or in the age to come' (Matt. 12:22–28, 29–32).

The 'unforgivable sin' is unbelief. Blind unbelief. Defiant unbelief. Unbelief in the face of overwhelming evidence in favour of belief. Unbelief that is blasphemous because it looks the sacred squarely in the face and profanes it through knowing, consistent, unalterable denial. In this context, specifically, it is unbelief that insists on attributing to Satan the work of the Holy Spirit.

When the Spirit descended like a dove upon Jesus at his baptism, the Son of Man was recognised as being the Son of God. His miracles, then, were a signature of the power of the Holy Spirit to transform water to wine, storms to calm, hunger to fulfilment, disease to health, and death to life. God's power to transform spiritual life was then promised to every believer who follows Jesus in baptism. We hear it from the Apostle Peter on the day of Pentecost after Jesus's own death-to-life resurrection transformation. Himself filled with the Holy Spirit, Peter said to those who sought forgiveness of their sins:

> Repent and be baptised, every one of you, in the name of Jesus Christ for the forgiveness of your sins. *And you will receive the gift of the Holy Spirit* (Acts 2:38).

Denying the regenerative power of the Holy Spirit leaves the sceptic *untransformed* – without peace, unfulfilled, spiritually diseased and dead. It is a self-defeating refusal to believe. But going so far as actually to attribute the work of the Holy Spirit to Satan – especially in the

Son of Man – was in yet a different category. More than simply being a personal *refusal* of the truth, it was a conscious, deliberate *reversal* of the truth! Beyond stubborn unbelief, it was callous *contempt*!

The Profanity of Refusing God's Grace

In a larger sense, of course, blasphemy against the Spirit is an unwillingness to acknowledge God and his Spirit of grace which saves us through Jesus Christ. If a person will not accept God's grace, there is no further remedy for his sin. No formula for forgiveness. No method of mercy. Its blasphemy arises from the impudence of refusing God's overture of love, as if man could save himself. It puts man in the driver's seat rather than God. It wrests the power of the Spirit from his hands into ours.

Look what Jesus seems to be telling us about our limited notion of *legal* blasphemy: 'Anyone who speaks a word against the Son of Man will be forgiven.' You mean that the editor of *Gay News* can be forgiven for his blasphemy against Jesus? Yes. Unconditionally? No. As with all sin, forgiveness is predicated upon belief and repentance. A genuine, obedient turning to God leads to forgiveness, no matter how heinous the offence – even if it is blasphemy against the Son of God.

The Apostle Paul knew it was true. He, himself, was a forgiven blasphemer against Christ.

> I thank Christ Jesus our Lord, who has given me strength, that he considered me faithful, appointing me to his service. Even though I was once a blasphemer and a persecutor and a violent man, I was shown mercy because I acted in ignorance and unbelief. The grace of our Lord was poured out on

me abundantly, along with the faith and love that are in Christ Jesus.

Here is a trustworthy saying that deserves full acceptance: Christ Jesus came into the world to save sinners – of whom I am the worst. But for that very reason I was shown mercy so that in me, the worst of sinners, Christ Jesus might display his unlimited patience as an example for those who would believe on him and receive eternal life (1 Tim. 1:12–16).

It's the flip side of God's offer of forgiveness that brings us to an even broader application of the 'unforgivable sin'. If we contemptuously refuse to accept God's offer, then forgiveness will not be forced upon us. Because salvation is found in Christ alone, denying Christ as our Lord and Saviour makes it impossible for God to save us. There is no other Way. There is no other Truth. There is no other Life.

Unthinkable Consequences of Blasphemy

Nobody likes a 'negative campaign', especially if it loses elections, but sometimes the hard truth has to be told as it is. In that spirit, the truth of God is that a day of judgment is coming. It will not be a test of who voted for whom in the Euro-elections, or whether we supported sanctions for South Africa, or even whether we participated in Holy Communion every Sunday in the local church. The test will be whether we have done honour to Christ by submitting our doctrine and our lives to his lordship; whether we have opened ourselves to the power of the Holy Spirit to transform us from within; whether we have served our fellow human beings with true righteousness and justice.

If we haven't met this level of commitment and service, then all the gushy talk about love and forgiveness in the world of religion will not save us from the wrath of our Creator. The Hebrew Christians might well share with us the warning they received: 'It is a dreadful thing to fall into the hands of the living God.'

In a time when hell is but a common swearword, I realise that these words approach the status of melodrama. The whole idea of judgment and hell seems somehow out-of-date, surreal, unsophisticated, anti-intellectual. Yet there it is, tumbling from Jesus's own lips: 'Do not be afraid of those who kill the body but cannot kill the soul. Rather, be afraid of the One who can destroy both soul and body in hell' (Matt. 10:28).

These tough words hardly seem consistent with the syrupy way in which Jesus is portrayed by today's clergy. Yet there is even more:

> Whoever acknowledges me before men, I will also acknowledge him before my Father in heaven. But whoever disowns me before men, I will disown him before my Father in heaven (Matt. 10:32–3).

How we regard Jesus of Nazareth is serious business. Whether Christian or Muslim, whether Church of England or Baptist, whether clergy or laity – we all need to engage in a careful and prayerful rethink of the unbelievable, yet undeniable Jesus – the man who performed incredible miracles and talked of life after death. The man who proved his power over death through his own resurrection. Yet the man who warns us that eternal life after death is not a promise to those who reject his lordship in their lives.

There is a blasphemy which can lead to threats of death in this life. Given obedient faith and repentance, it is a forgivable blasphemy, even if the body is destroyed. However, we must make no mistake about it. There is also an unforgivable blasphemy, a type which leads to eternal destruction of the soul. Jesus could not have put it more forcefully:

> You are from below; I am from above. You are of this world; I am not of this world. I told you that you would die in your sins; if you do not believe that I am the one I claim to be, you will indeed die in your sins (John 8:23–4).

Are we spiritual Rushdies, attempting to hide from God's righteous judgment? Have we blasphemed him with defiant unbelief? If so, we can always run, but never hide.

We can also do the simpler thing, the more loving thing. We can admit that we have acted contemptuously, and humbly reach out for God's forgiveness.

Jesus, the Great Profaner

There is a wonderful sense in which Jesus truly was the greatest profaner of all time. Although he never committed blasphemy against the genuinely sacred, he did indeed profane all of this world's 'sacred cows'. He took the world's value system and totally restructured it. What we consider to be important, he turned upside down.

In doing that, of course, Jesus constantly offended sensibilities, including religious tradition. He took a radical, even revolutionary, attitude to all that was human and, especially, hypocritical.

From a *human* viewpoint, it was 'blasphemy' to be the Messiah, yet not a member of the clergy, or from the wealthy class or the highly educated. It was 'blasphemy' to choose ordinary men as his special apostles. It was 'blasphemy' to treat women with dignity, to reach out to the Gentiles, to honour the poor – and most offensive of all – to die on a cross! In refusing to honour the conventions and prejudices of his day, Jesus was guilty of social sacrilege.

In the eyes of the world, then and now, Jesus was a blasphemer! It is no wonder that we try to get rid of him every way we can. With that troublemaker around how can we get on with what we want to do?

Luckily for us, we can't get rid of him. Luckily for us, he treats with divine contempt the insignificant and distorted human values we hold on to so tightly. Our values *need* to be stirred. Our priorities *need* to be turned upside down. Our unholy 'sacred cows' *need* to be profaned.

Praise God for blaspheming all that is unworthy within us!

15

Towards a Godly Intolerance

Protesting Blasphemy Through Lives Devoted to Christ

> May His spirit divine all my being refine,
> Let the beauty of Jesus be seen in me.
> George L. Johnson

We began this book with reference to the outcry by Muslims over the Salman Rushdie affair. For virtually all Muslims, Rushdie's book was blasphemous and, to most, worthy of death. To the Christian community in Britain, such religious fanaticism belongs to another era altogether, if not to another world. Yet concurrent with the Rushdie affair was the surprisingly parallel 'Mackay affair' – not at all Muslim in character, but very much Christian.

In case it slipped anyone's attention, Lord Chancellor Mackay of Clashfern was excommunicated and stripped of his office of eldership by the Free Presbyterian Church. The offence? Mackay's attendance at Roman Catholic requiem masses for Lord Russell of Killowan and Lord Wheatley, both legal colleagues and friends of the Lord Chancellor. Are you still looking for the offence? I'm afraid that's all there is: mere attendance at a Roman Catholic mass! 'But the deceased were professional colleagues,' you say. Doesn't matter. 'And they were personal friends.' It doesn't matter. 'Surely Lord Mackay doesn't approve of the Catholic mass.' It still doesn't matter.

What to others seems the most improbable kind of ruling was explained by Donald MacLean, Clerk of the Southern Presbytery:

> I find it very difficult to believe that the Lord Chancellor of a Protestant country, with a Protestant queen on a Protestant throne, has any obligation by reason of state to go to a Popish mass. It is the highest form of worship in the Roman Catholic church and it is idolatrous and blasphemous.

There we have it again, the word *blasphemy*! Like love, blasphemy seems to cover a multitude of sins. One wonders, of course, if the Free Presbyterians feel so much closer an affinity with the high Anglo-Catholic Church of England that their funeral services would have been viewed more sympathetically. Is 'Protestantism' sufficient to draw the line between blasphemy and non-blasphemy?

Moreover, what would the Free Presbyterians say of Jesus's eating and drinking with the publicans and sinners of his day? Would they join with the Pharisees to point an accusing finger at Jesus and to tell him he's fraternising with those who blaspheme? I suspect his case would be distinguished on the basis that Jesus had an exclusive prerogative as the Son of God, or, perhaps, as involving an act which would not be considered blasphemous in itself. Nevertheless, the compassion shown by Jesus for non-believers must cause even the

Free Presbyterians to feel uneasy about their decision in the Lord Chancellor's case.

A Matter of Intolerance

Fundamentalists (such an ill-defined term!), whether Christian or Muslim, share a common characteristic, which is intolerance for dissent, acted or spoken. Intolerance is a means of maintaining a system of dogma. I am not so sure, however, that it can be understood solely by Charles James Fox's analysis that 'the only foundation for tolerance is a degree of scepticism'. Surely a person can have certain doubts about his own beliefs while at the same time drawing strict lines of intolerance at the point of another's disbelief. At some point, all of us draw lines which show the limits of our tolerance. When we do so, we are deciding the things about which we must be *intolerant*.

The role of intolerance is to prevent the seemingly-inevitable drift from fundamentalism to liberalism. (It never seems to *drift* in the other direction.) Let the door be cracked open just a little, and the winds of liberalism are likely to blow it wide open. Open the floodgate of scepticism the slightest bit, and soon there will be a deluge of doubt. Set yourself on a slippery slope of higher Biblical criticism and watch how soon you are on a downhill slide to disbelief. Allow the thin end of the wedge to be driven into Church tradition, and before you know it the tree of faithfulness has been felled.

Consider how often we operate on the basis of similar 'floodgate-type' concerns in secular matters and you begin to appreciate why seemingly-arbitrary lines are often drawn regarding religious matters. In the religious arena, a church cannot remain strong without a godly intolerance for unorthodox teaching, as it defines orthodoxy. The doctrinal tolerance and spirit of accommodation of which the Anglican fellowship has been so proud has served only to usher the Church into dangerous decline. To quote a now-familiar source (Salman Rushdie), 'Compromise is the temptation of the weak' (p. 467).

If you have never before made the connection, usually it is *fundamentalists* who wear the label of being intolerant. By definition, fundamentalists are always closer to the 'fundamentals' of a given religion and, typically, have undergone recent 'revolutions' to restore the basics. I don't know of a single instance where liberalism was restored to 'fundamentals' through a gradual process of change. It must be achieved through a process of throwing off (often through forceful confrontation) the institutionalism and laxness of the liberalism from which its predecessor has evolved.

Therefore, it should not be surprising that, once the 'revolution' is successfully in place, intolerance will prevail. Where the battle to regain lost territory was hard fought, no ground will be given. Why conquer the enemy, only to let down your guard? At any sign of crumbling – whether in doctrine, culture, or in some instances the language which holds that culture together – intolerance becomes the first line of defence. You see it in a Muslim people struggling to maintain moral purity in the face of Western immorality. You see it in the beleaguered (only 6,000-strong) Free Presbyterians, many of whom are part of a threatened Gaelic culture in the Western Isles of Scotland.

In each instance the cry is: better intolerant and intact than tolerant and torn apart. On doctrinal issues, they have good cause for taking such a stand. We only need look to the doctrinal and ethical laxity on the part of the Church of England to see what happens when lines of tolerance are bent so far that they break. Whoever could have guessed twenty years ago how far the Church would have tolerated homosexual activity? Or changes in the role of women in the appointive leadership of the Church? Or recognition of divorce?

Tolerance Not a Christian Virtue

This may seem shocking, but tolerance has never been a Christian virtue. You don't even find the word in the Bible. What you find are words like 'contend for the faith that was once for all entrusted to the saints' (Jude 3). And 'watch out for those who cause divisions and put obstacles in your way that are contrary to the teaching you have learned. Keep away from them' (Rom. 16:17). And 'Expel the wicked man from among you . . . hand this man over to Satan, so that the sinful nature may be destroyed and his spirit saved on the day of the Lord (1 Cor. 5:13, 5). And, 'Among [those denying the faith] are Hymenaeus and Alexander, whom I have handed over to Satan to be taught not to blaspheme' (1 Tim. 1:20). Those are not the words of tolerance, but of intolerance.

Yet we must be careful not to equate intolerance towards doctrinal error or moral irresponsibility with insensitivity towards the individuals involved. For example, Jesus did not join in the stoning of the woman caught in adultery (John 7:53–8:11). While he did not tolerate her sin ('Go now and leave your life of sin.'), Jesus had compassion on her ('Neither do I condemn you'). Jesus was hard on issues and soft on people. (Any exception to that rule was his unrelenting harshness with religious leaders, whom Jesus saw as the greatest threat to doctrinal purity.)

The Apostle Paul also found room to manoeuvre on *behavioural* or *cultural* issues when successful evangelism of the Gospel was the greater good.

To the Jews I became like a Jew, to win the Jews.

> To those under the law I became like one under the law (though I myself am not under the law), so as to win those under the law. To those not having the law I became like one not having the law (though I am not free from God's law but am under Christ's law), so as to win those not having the law. To the weak I became weak, to win the weak.
>
> I have become all things to all men so that by all possible means I might save some (1 Cor. 9:20–2).

In making this concession for the sake of the Gospel, Paul was neither tolerant in one extreme, nor hypocritical in the opposite extreme. He was simply meeting unbelievers where they were, accommodating them where he found common ground. In defence of the truth against religious error as we understand it to be, we must avoid the temptation to waffling, weak-willed tolerance. Yet if we are not to *tolerate*, we must never fail to *appreciate* where we can.

My own judgment is that the Free Presbyterians failed to see the difference in the case of the Lord Chancellor. Intractably fixed on maintaining doctrinal purity, they were not sensitive to the bereaved, or to Paul's teaching that Christians are to 'mourn with those who mourn' (Rom. 12:15). In short, they chose the wrong enemy and the wrong battleground.

On the other hand, if given a choice between those who stand up for their beliefs – at the risk of taking intolerance over the top – and those for whom truth is too politically hot to handle or too mysterious to know or defend, then give me those who care about Biblical teaching! With those who respect the Scriptures, I still have a chance to appeal to their consciences, and I share with them a common basis of appeal.

It's time, also, to explode a popular myth. At the end of the day, you will find intolerance at *both* extremes. Hardly ever is there a more intolerant person

Towards a Godly Intolerance

than the intellectually liberal religious sort. For he will tolerate anything and anyone other than that which might get in the way of his own liberalism, at which point loving ecumenism turns into self-righteous outrage against unthinking, close-minded, so-called unenlightened fundamentalism. For the intellectual liberal Christian, homosexuality can be tolerated under the banner of Christian 'love', but not excommunication in the name of doctrinal purity.

Intolerance a Product of Seriousness

If none of this makes sense to you, if you think the action of the Free Presbyterians was obsolete and absurd, then you probably don't have the kind of faith that they have. Yet, surprisingly, if you are outraged by what they did to Lord Mackay, then you may feel something of how *they* felt, misguided as you think their feelings may have been. Can we tolerate in others the feelings that we ourselves have about them?

And what of the Rushdie affair? If you are outraged by the death threat against Salman Rushdie, perhaps you can begin to feel something of what *Muslims* felt, misguided as you think their feelings may have been. Again, can we tolerate in others the feeling that we ourselves have about them?

Appreciation is a two-way street, but not always a free ride. Appreciating the feelings of others doesn't mean we can't speak out against injustice. It doesn't mean we can't point out the incongruity of the Free Presbyterian Church's failure to maintain respectful decorum in a meeting designed to maintain doctrinal purity. (The Lord Chancellor's trial ended with scenes of rancour and dissension.) It doesn't mean we can't point out the overriding sanctity of life to those Muslims who would kill Rushdie for offending their faith, or worse yet in some Islamic societies, kill those who would be baptised into Christ.

What it *does* mean is that we must learn to appreciate those who stand up for their beliefs, and to question ourselves as to whether we value anything enough in our own lives to kill or be killed because of it. If we should not kill another person under any circumstances, is there anything at all that we should *die* for? Would that include our religious beliefs? Would it be religious beliefs wholly apart from cultural conflict (so as to exclude the 'religious' strife in Northern Ireland)?

Oliver Leaman (*The Times*, February 6th, 1989) addressed the issue regarding both Muslims and the Free Presbyterians and lauded those who take religion seriously:

> What we have here yet again is a group of people who take their religion seriously, and who are prepared to react angrily when they feel their religion is being attacked. The rest of us are unable to see what all the fuss is about precisely because there is a deep tradition in Britain which refuses to take religion seriously, and which merely sees it as a matter of personal belief, on a par with the colour of socks one prefers to wear or the television programmes one chooses to watch.
>
> We must try to grasp that unusual phenomenon in our society, the person who takes religion seriously.

The real question becomes, then, how strong is our faith? How seriously do we take our own religion? Is blasphemy a non-issue to us because our sense of the sacred has been numbed? Blasphemy and intolerance are first cousins. They are lines which are drawn to maintain sacredness and faith by people who take religion seriously. If nothing is sacred, blasphemy is impossible!

Pluralism and Intolerance

The obvious question at this point is, How can we exercise 'Christian intolerance' in a pluralistic society? When does accommodation to sincere differences and sensitivity to the consciences of others cross the line from faith-guarded intolerance to wishy-washy, all-is-acceptable tolerance? When does the failure to protest weaken our resolve? On the other hand, when does our own line-drawing violate the rights of others to proceed in good faith in a different direction? Perhaps it is too simplistic to suggest that Jesus has led the way, saying, 'Do to others as you would have them do to you.'

In the case of Lord Mackay, who presumably agrees with the Church's basic stand against Roman Catholicism, I can see where application of the 'golden rule' might lead to greater understanding and less hardened bigotry on the part of the Church. In Rushdie's case, by contrast, I don't get the feeling that his disbelief could ever have engendered sufficient goodwill among Muslims for the 'golden rule' to have come into force. It was his very disbelief that brought on the blasphemy. Perhaps the same could be said of Martin Scorsese's *Last Temptation of Christ*.

What are the available options, then, when confronted by blasphemy on the part of those who do not share one's faith? I should think it elementary, first of all, that any form of violence must be ruled out. If Muslims would disagree, I should suggest in that difference alone Christianity shows itself superior to Islam. Violence does not bring honour to God.

It is not a sign of moral weakness or secular seduction to denounce the use of violence in the promotion of religious faith. In the person of Christ, God would not even defend himself from arrest, trial and death on a cross. To Peter, who had drawn a sword in the garden where Jesus was arrested, Jesus said, 'Put your sword back in its place, for all who draw the sword will die by the sword' (Matt. 26:52).

Short of violence, there may be protest vocally and in print against those who would blaspheme the name of God. We ought to have as much righteous outrage against moral and spiritual desecration as we do against social and political injustice. If we can protest against nuclear bombers at Greenham Common, then we can and must protest whatever would destroy us as a nation *spiritually*. If we can protest against separation between blacks and whites in South Africa, then we can and must protest at the failure to *distinguish* between moral 'black and white' in such issues as homosexuality and divorce.

In each instance, of course, we shall have to judge whether we have chosen the right battle to fight. Will our protests serve only to widen the blasphemy? Shall we give more notice to the blasphemy than it deserves? Worse yet, are we creating the possibility that peaceful protest (a good witness to the world) will turn into violent confrontation (an affront to the Lord of Peace)? 'Prayerful Discretion Now!' should be the first banner we paint.

Time to Cleanse the Temple

First and foremost, of course, we must clean up our own house. How can we expect to be a witness to the secular world if we have not first rid ourselves of a secularised church? If heresy does not fall under criminal blasphemy laws (and it should not), it *does* fall within the responsibility of the Church to root out and eradicate. There is Biblical precedent – no, *mandate* – for the withdrawal of fellowship from Christian leaders who blaspheme Scripture through wholesale distribution of doubt:

> What business is it of mine to judge those outside the church? Are you not to judge those inside? God will judge those outside. 'Expel the wicked man from among you' (1 Cor. 5:12–13).

It's not just the Bishop of Durham, who certainly is a prime example. It's also the former Bishop of Birmingham, Hugh Montefiore, whose book *The Probability of God* (SCM Press, 1985), was a disingenuous – even blasphemous – attempt to reconcile scientific evolutionary thought with Biblical teaching concerning sin and salvation. (*Sin*, the result of a human brain which, like the horns of the Irish elk, over-evolved? *Soul*, simply the independent consciousness of the self, apart from the material brain?)

If this sounds like a call for a purge within the Church, then a purge let it be! To purge is to cleanse. The Church needs a bloodbath of truth in the Saviour's blood to wash it clean from the stain of sceptics. Let them say what they wish to say in the name of free speech, but not while wearing the cloak of the Church!

I can well appreciate how inflammatory and un-Christian this language must appear to some. Yet sometime, somehow, in some way we must come to appreciate the degree of spiritual danger into which sceptical religious leaders have led a nation already suffering from a crisis in faith. Paul pulled no punches:

> But even if we or an angel from heaven should preach a gospel other than the one we preached to you, let him be eternally condemned! As we have already said, so now I say again: If anybody is preaching to you a gospel other than what you accepted, let him be eternally condemned (Gal. 1: 8–9).

How else are we to turn it around? One could wish, at a minimum, that stronger voices of dissent could be heard from among other leaders in the Church. Is there a conspiracy of silence among the fraternity of fellow bishops? Will they speak out against non-Church sceptics, but treat with kid gloves those who are members of the club?

Is it, God forbid, that there is none left who disagree? If so, then it is *God* who will do the purging. Perhaps he will let the Church drift into oblivion so that he can then raise up a Church of strength and faith and obedience. Considering the waning influence of the Church, perhaps God's purge has already begun. Stand fast, all you who are among the faithful remnant. In God's own time, his Church will be restored in Britain!

The Purge Within

When it comes to solving Britain's spiritual crisis, however, it is too easy to target the Bishop of Durham (who represents a Church unwilling to stand firm for the Truth) or Salman Rushdie (who represents a secular world out of touch with all that is sacred) as the reason for our problems. In spiritual matters, the problem always begins with us – each one of us, one by one.

It is too easy to say that we aren't guilty of blasphemy under Britain's blasphemy laws or that we don't commit heresy by abusing the written Word of God. Do we not blaspheme God's name in our speech and in our actions? Have we profaned the sacred by failing to see how our day-to-day materialism competes with true Christian teaching? Are we under condemnation for our insipid, uninspired, and tepid Christianity?

It is altogether possible that we might speak out against David Jenkins's denial of Jesus's physical

Towards a Godly Intolerance 221

resurrection, yet fail to show our neighbours the risen Christ spiritually living within us. We might well decry the ever-weakening moral foundation in Britain, yet fail to rid our own lives of those sins which we know are an affront to God. We may indeed get outraged about the death threat to Salman Rushdie, yet fail to see how our own racial prejudice against British Muslims has increased as a result.

Intolerance must begin within ourselves. We must no longer tolerate our own sin and prejudice and spiritual laxness. Protest must be in the heart – against our own hypocrisy, our own lack of faith, our own pretensions. Only then can we make a difference in a world of indifference. Only then will those of other faiths come to respect what we stand for and the God in whom we place our trust. Only then shall we bring true honour to God and restore in this nation a sense of the sacred.

Lord, purge from within each of us the blasphemies that cause others to turn away from you. Cleanse us of our own sin that we might call others to purity. Instil within us a sense of seriousness about our faith, that we no longer be Christians in name only, but in word and in deed and, above all, in your Truth.